Silk, Spices, Veils and Vodka

by Felicity Timcke

Published in United Kindom
Hertforfshire Press © 2014
(Imprint of Silk Road Media)

Suite 125, 43 Bedford Street
Covent Garden, London
WC2 9HA United Kingdom
www.hertfordshirepress.com

Silk, Spices, Veils and Vodka
by Felicity Timcke

Typeset by Aleksandra Vlasova

British Library Catalogue in Publication Data
A catalogue record for this book is available from the British Library
Library of Congress in Publication Data
A catalogue record for this book has been requested

ISBN 978-0-9927873-1-8

Contents

To Wendy, who re-typed the lost manuscript

About the Author

Felicity Timcke was born, grew up and was educated in South Africa with a Bachelor of Music, a Post Graduate Diploma in Information Science, a Bachelor of English Literature and Language Arts and an Honorary Doctorate in the Theory and Practice of Languages. She chose to travel the world with her husband, Michael, whose work took them to some very exotic places, mostly along the Silk Road, keeping herself busy with her passions: music and languages. She continues to travel the world, not committing to any other place but South Africa as her home. Michael, her greatest supporter and critic, has made some contributions to the text in this book.

Living and working away from home, while it may sound glamorous, is not always an easy lifestyle, nevertheless, it remains an interesting one. This book is dedicated to all my loyal friends and loving family members especially, who made it so much easier for me, through their constant loving friendship and concern, the letters, Skype and e-mails, the gifts, their flexibility in terms of accommodation and visits, the lending of cars, sofas, spare rooms, spontaneous meals at restaurants, random meetings at airports, and much, much more...... like pretending to like the gaudy souvenirs I would bring back every Christmas from far flung places with no taste in handicrafts...

Most of all, thank you for pretending that the hundreds of "goodbyes" were not as difficult as they really were. If they were anything like my "goodbyes", then I know how hard it was.

I love you

Twenty Years of Musings

It has been brought to my attention that Michael and I have been bouncing around Central Asia and Europe for more than 20 years. Believe it or not, this came as a surprise to me. I feel like I am still "getting used to being away from home". After much thought, I think I can attribute this "wandering spirit" to my late father, who, as a young boy of 17, left his home in the North of Holland soon after the war. After encounters in Ukraine, Poland, Germany and Russia, he returned only for a while before joining a ship full of fortune-seekers bound for deepest, darkest Africa. Upon arriving in South Africa, with only the telephone number of a relative who was supposed to "pave the way", he forged his path under many guises, the most colourful being a strawberry farmer and a yoghurt-maker. Unlike his wandering daughter, once settled, he never moved again. I used to love sitting on his veranda during my visits home, sharing my stories, embellishing them to make them more attractive, waiting for his reactions – usually surprisingly interested, sometimes horrified, but most times involved, evident through his large map of the world on the wall of his workroom used to make the necessary references with coloured pins and pieces of string marking the places I have visited and their distance from home.. such was my Dad.

My mother's daring, never-say-no approach to life also contributed to my inability to allow the fear of the unknown to scare me away from trying new things. "Apply for this", "go for that", "you will be able to do it, don't worry", were phrases that pushed me through accompanying an entire operetta production on the piano at the age of 13, driving a VW Beetle from Nelspruit to Johannesburg on my own at the age of 17 (during the petrol sanction of the 1980s), and shipping me off to Australia as an exchange student for a year of giving speeches about how wonderful South Africa was in 1983. This was good practice for trying out new things.

My parents' influence, coupled with the insatiable adventurous spirit of my life partner and also my best friend, collectively, Michael and I have been to more than 50 countries, and lived in eight. While this may sound like everyone's dream, believe me, traveling is not glamorous at all!! On the contrary, it can be quite stressful, time-consuming and very tiring. Looking back though, I have learned a few things…

My first trip ever was to England and then to the island of Cyprus. I was going to be there for six months, so it straddled over two seasons. Therefore, I had to pack for both winter and summer. England, according to uninformed-never-travelled-before little me, did not have any shops, and with the British Pound to South African Rand exchanging at 11:1 – shopping for any extras was out of the question. EVERYTHING had to be packed, stuffed and miraculously squeezed into my suitcase. The suitcases of 20 years ago were not nearly as strong and sturdy as today's, neither did they have convenient storage pockets for small items such as underwear and the like. They also didn't have wheels!!! Upon arrival at the airport in London, to my horror, out came my belongings…. not in the suitcase, but individually on the carousel which lazily wound round, and round, and round again... I had to painfully watch as one pair of knickers, followed by another, and another, then a shoe, a sock and then the entire suitcase burst open at the seams, unfolded before my eyes, giving each and every passenger on my flight a good look at the contents of my overstuffed suitcase. Did I claim the suitcase…? Of course! With the Pound at 11:1, I simply had to!

What did I learn? Pack your knickers in the secret compartment hidden in the lid of the suitcase so it will only be your shoes and clothes on the carousel when the suitcase explodes.

On the subject of packing suitcases and knickers: as I continued to travel and become a more experienced packer, I can now fit my entire life into ten suitcases (including bedside lamps, photo-frames and 62 pairs of shoes). I worked out, over the years, that if one packed one's dirty laundry on the top, then most customs officials are reluctant to rummage through one's luggage. This worked perfectly until one day I was stopped by a Mozambican official at the airport in Maputo. He was armed with white gloves and a stick that looked very much like an orchestra conductor's baton. He proceeded to "flick" through my luggage with his baton, strewing my pretty little g-strings all over the floor like confetti at a wedding. Packing your underwear on top is not a good idea after all.

Living in a variety of hotels, while it may seem luxurious, can also be a challenge. Not having a home of my own has, over the years, taught me to put down roots almost immediately. On arriving in a hotel room, I am able, within the first hour, to transform it into a home. My habit is to first get rid of all unnecessary and ugly decorations. I usually stuff them into one of the cupboards. I have been known to take pictures off the walls and hide them away along with the unsightly ornaments in a dark cupboard that is not being used! I then move the furniture to where it's most functional. I set up a charging station for the many mobile phones, computers and iPods we drag along with us. An important element for me is background music, so out come the portable speakers and the iPod. If the room is drab, then I head for the nearest shop for a bunch of flowers.

What have I learned from this? Always carry a pretty cloth in your suitcase in case the bed-cover or the upholstery of the chair is ugly. Mind you, given the countries we visit, beautiful cloths and even carpets are easy to find, so redecorating a hotel room is not all that difficult.

Another essential is the snack station which caters for all tastes in the food and drink area. Use the mini bar? NEVER! I'm far too stingy for that. And who wants to eat little bags of nuts and drink club soda anyway? Finding the nearest shop and smuggling in bags of snacks past the bell boy can be a challenge, but it is worth-while once the munchies hit at midnight when your body-clock hits breakfast time.

Food is always a challenge when visiting new countries. My rule of thumb is to eat everything local. There is nothing worse than a vegetarian McDonald's burger in India or a pizza in a place like Uzbekistan where they make cheese that doesn't melt. Local is good.

What have I learned? If an entire country can eat it, then so can you, even if it is sheep's testicles fried in butter and onions.

What about language? This remains a challenge. My strategy, being the extrovert actor that I am, is to learn a few key words and phrases and throw them out at the right moment. This will impress the local listener no end, politely saying "Ha, you speak Russian perfectly!!!" Coming across as "knowing the language" will get you into places, give you discounts, cups of tea and free taxi rides. Of course, knowing too much could get you into trouble, especially if you don't know enough language to get you out of trouble.

What have I learned? Language is directly connected to the soul. A little effort goes a long way towards winning the respect of people. I am currently feverishly trying to learn Persian. My problem is the script – all the language-learning books I find require one to learn Arabic script and I am in far too much of a hurry to do that. I want to speak the language and I want to speak it now. I finally found a book in a hotel called "Simple Colloquial Persian without writing it". Perfect for me. It was written by an Englishman who worked for the Anglo-Iranian Oil Company in Abadan in 1937, printed in 1937 and revised in 1941. The 22 simple lessons have given me quite a lot of insight into the mechanics of the grammar but unfortunately, I am stuck with useful phrases such as:

"Why do you hit the donkey?"

"Why do you hit me? I am not a thief, I am your friend."

"The day before yesterday I sat here from morning until night".

And my most useful phrase so far, "The line which they drew between the office and the post office is crooked."

It reminds me of the Uzbek I learned from my cello teacher. I ended up with useful phrases such as "relax your left arm", "the bow must be

12

straight". And so on.

One thing I am eternally thankful for is that South Africa was colonized by the British and not the Portuguese, or the Germans, or the French. Without this little perk in my country's life (I have chosen to ignore the negative aspects of this part of our history), I have managed to find myself work all over the world using English – the proverbial "goose that lays the golden egg". With my educational background in Music, Information Science and English Literature and Language, coupled with my confidence and *chutzpa* (the Yiddish word for "audacity"), I have found countless interesting jobs ranging from English teaching, stylistic editing, a hotel receptionist, and even a journalist.

I was once asked by Forbes Magazine to write a feature article on "Business Investment Opportunities in Uzbekistan". What deserved to be a one-page article or less owing to the dire lack of business opportunities, turned out to be an article of about 30 pages which pleased the people from Forbes until I was accused of plagiarism. Apparently I had plagiarized one of my own books! Earlier, I had written an annual economic review for the Ministry of Economic Development of Uzbekistan but was not allowed to use my own name because I was not a local writer… Therefore, I ended up "stealing my own words". With such limited information available on the topic, it was a question of "how many ways to skin a cat" if you are familiar with that idiom. The article was never printed.

My music background has enabled me to sing in many choirs, play instruments in ensembles and even orchestrate a road trip, organizing a tour of concerts for a string quartet from Uzbekistan to visit South Africa and Mozambique. The best two weeks of my life must be the road trip I did with these four musicians and their instruments all stuffed into my Toyota Rav4, hurtling through Southern Africa. I was the driver, public relations consultant, fund-raiser, translator and Master of Ceremonies all rolled into one. The musicians were a motley crew of Uzbeks, Russians and Uighurs (check the Internet), scared to death to come to deepest, darkest Africa. In an attempt to calm themselves before concerts, they resorted to the vodka-drinking habits of the USSR, accompanied by pickled cucumbers and cigarettes before and after every concert. Upon arriving at each destination, we would unpack their tuxedos, bowties, black dresses, shiny shoes and instruments, decide who would sleep where, put together and programme for the concert and then drink vodka, eat pickled cucumbers and smoke…. I was always amazed how quickly and how well they "cleaned up" before a concert – and literally only minutes before the curtain was about to rise. Many times I would be on the stage introducing them and announcing the programme for the evening not knowing if what was waiting behind the curtains was "ready" or not. Sometimes I would even say a piece had ended even if it was between the 3rd movement and the finale. How was I supposed to know? Needless to say, they stole the hearts of their audiences at every one of the fourteen concerts we did during those two weeks.

My two most memorable moments were in Maputo: the first being showing them the sea for the very first time (Uzbekistan is a double land-locked country and is nowhere near the sea). The second was sitting in the art-deco building of what used to be Maputo Train Station (now a very hip and trendy jazz venue) jamming with Mozambican musicians until the sun came up. Most of these musicians were from Maputo and, although excellent instrumentalists in their own right, had never set eyes on a real violin, cello or viola, let alone jam with them. Some moments are so precious they can only be remembered, never relived.

Michael's diplomatic sojourn taught me countless social skills. I can hold a glass of wine and a plate of eats while balancing on stilettos, keeping trivial conversation with the Ambassador of Poland's wife, or the Cultural Attaché of Serbia or… or…or…. Prince Charles! I can chat with the most boring people and look interested even if they are the driest conversationalists ever. I can scan a room full of pretentious people and make a mental note of the most interesting and "useful" people to target, and then meet my target by the end of a cocktail party. The target is "working the crowd", that is, getting to know people who are mutually beneficial in any given circumstance. I can make bite-sized canapés, and set a table with the cloth hanging symmetrically – even lengths on all sides! I can remember people's names, mostly, and subtly convince people I know their names when introducing them, even if I don't. A carefully honed skill.

What I learned: when hosting your own function, such as a National Day, do not drink wine or Champagne from the outset. On the first National Day that we hosted, I kept drinking our imported South African wines with the guests, taking a fresh glass every time the waiter handed me one. After the first hour I was quite tipsy, not acceptable for the hostess of a diplomatic function... an evening I prefer to forget. I now know that apple juice looks like wine – nurse it, pretend it is the real thing, and leave the best until the end.

Being a lover of fashion and a follower of style, clothing has always been the bane of my multi-cultural existence, especially living in the countries we have chosen to live in. I love my hair, and I love my spikey hairstyle! Yet, every day, no matter how much blow drying, styling and heavy-duty hair gel I devote to my hair, it all ends up in a flat mess under a head covering. With no acceptable hairstyle to rely on, I have discovered the art of make-up. This is a vital accessory, including beautiful fingernails and toes. Boy, can Iranian women flirt with their eyes and their toes! I can now confidently answer the question: "If you were stranded on a desert island and could take one thing with you what would it be?" "LIPSTICK, of course!"

What have I learned? I will NEVER look like a local. Some travellers try to dress like the people in the country they are visiting or living in. While in some countries' local attire may work, one really needs to draw the line at donning baggy trousers, wearing a nose-ring and cultivating dreadlocks. Trying to dress like a local will not help when trying to blend in. There is something about a person's walk, posture and of course facial features that somehow gives a foreigner away – in any country. Of course, for me it's my big bum. My bum will always stand out as a foreign-feature and oh, how I love going home to Africa to find my big bum can actually turn a head or two...

Religion and politics are two things I will not discuss in detail.

What have I learned about these two important areas of Life? Curiosity and understanding are two virtues I have developed more than any others. The world is a small place and the majority end up thinking the same as you. It just takes time to listen to what people have to say, and effort to understand how they think. If this happens, then tolerance requires no effort at all.

Last, but definitely not least, are friends. It takes time to make friends and effort to keep them. Making a friend and being able to maintain a relationship over many miles and many years is an art and not many can do this. To not see someone for years and then meet and effortlessly pick up a relationship is a gift many of our friends have. We are and should be eternally grateful for this gift.

What do I call "home"? I always ask myself this question. All I can say is when we use the phrase "the world is a global village" flippantly; it means more than that to me.

In the following pages I have complied some of the letters I wrote to friends and family worldwide. These are my impressions, experiences, feelings and frustrations. I hope this will serve as an insightful journey into the lands many may never get to see and meet the people many may never get to meet.

Letters From Uzbekistan
My World of "firsts"

Dear Friends,

A Salaam Alekum, Greetings from Uzbekistan – the land of Marco Polo and Genghis Khan. All our vain imaginings dissolved into reality as we stepped off our airplane, bade farewell to our "bearded airhostess" only to face the initially scary, soon to become, annoying faces of Uzbekistan's border control officials. Despite what we anticipated, the flight on Uzbekistan Airways was surprisingly pleasant. As a welcome to the country, we were given what seemed, millions of forms we had to fill in about bringing American money into the country and about our jewellery and firearms and drugs......all on yellowed, very faintly printed paper, only in Russian, printed in Cyrillic, an alphabet I had NEVER set eyes on before. The customs officials, trying their hardest to look as mean, intimidating and unfriendly as possible, insisted on shoving our bursting suitcases through their x-ray machines, assuring us that our films and computers would be safe. Were they??? No!!!! Nothing could be safe passing through those rays – the machine was straight out of the 60's.

We were transported to our hotel in a bus way past its vintage, leaning over to one side, threatening to topple over as it turned each corner. Adding to the excitement was the excruciating sound of grinding gears, the nauseating smell of petrol fumes and frightening rattling of windows – not to forget the enormous spider-web crack right across the front windscreen.

Apparently the former city of Tashkent was destroyed by an earthquake in 1966 and has been rebuilt in the style of a modern Russian city with few traditional Muslim buildings left. Rumour has it that this earthquake really wasn't that devastating, it was merely a Soviet ploy to "pretend" that all the buildings were destroyed, providing an excuse to grow more hideous Soviet-looking nine-storey structures. Strangely enough, the religious areas with mosques were worst hit – while the old city, with falling-down mud and straw houses, still stands secure. Who knows? Who will ever know?

The streets are very wide, giving the appearance of very little traffic. All the cars on the road are Volgas (a Russian luxury car driven mostly by bureaucrats) and Ladas, a middle-of-the-range car that looks like a Fiat from the 60's. Buildings all look the same – it's difficult to distinguish between flats, shops, offices, although the odd house tucked between the multi-storey buildings is a bit of a give-away. The problem is compounded by the Cyrillic alphabet which is what all the signs are written in: a bread shop, for example, will be called "HOH" and a restaurant will be a "PECTOPAH" mmmmm...... Everyone speaks Russian while some Uzbeks speak Uzbek as well; others speak Tajik, Uighur, Kazakh and more. Although some are related, these are languages my ear has never heard before! I will be learning Uzbek, the language of independent Uzbekistan, related to Turkish.

Tashkent has a model metro system; spotlessly clean with a train every six minutes! Each metro station is beautifully decorated depicting a particular theme – for example the glorious cotton-growers of yore, the Poet Alisher Navoi (a poet from the 13th century who has become a cultural icon since Independence), the glories of Independence and more nostalgic and nationalistic expressions. The city also has an assortment of above ground public transportation including trolley-buses and trams built in the 1940s – something that managed to survive the war. Every car is a taxi, if it has four wheels it can be hailed – the inside may sometimes be a little dilapidated, for example a screwdriver holding up the window or a string holding the door closed – what the heck, it gets you from point A to point B at very little expense (that's if you can explain to the taxi driver where you want to go).

Back to our hotel, a very tall, unusual-looking cylindrical structure called the *Chorsu* Hotel. Registration took at least one hour, thousands of forms to fill in, in multiple copies (no carbon paper or photocopies). We had to part with our passports – the internal police; better known as the KGB, insisted on keeping them for the purpose of registration (I think it was to keep us under their watchful eyes and to hold us hostage in an "administrative" way).

The hotel room was far beyond our expectations: let me just say there was a bed with linen – the sheets were too small for the bed – a bathroom and a fridge – a very noisy fridge that made strange noises all night. There was also a multitude of six-legged unwanted guests as well as a very nosey "key manager" dressed in a white coat, thick socks and slippers who sat at her rickety desk at the end of the corridor insisting on knowing our every move. We found out later that the purpose of these "corridor ladies" was not to ensure we have a comfortable stay, but rather to watch our every move and report anything that may cause concern, including the shopping we brought in from outside, the company we kept and the hours we entered and exited the building. Although she did not seem to speak English, I was convinced after two days that she spoke fluent English and reported every conversation we had. Nevertheless, the noisy fridge, leaking tap and running toilet provided noisy interludes to the wild Uzbek music accompanying the festivities going on in the function room on the ground floor. I still wonder if she heard "everything".

We spent a few days of orientation in Tashkent – visiting the vibrant and colourful *Chorsu* Bazaar (bursting with the freshest, plumpest assortment of fruit and vegetables), attempting to cross a six-lane street with no traffic lights (a habit soon to become second-nature to us) and visiting the Uzbekistan History Museum that explained the intricacies of Darwin and his Theory of Evolution (in a Muslim country). Obviously changing the exhibits of the museum was not a priority since Independence from the Soviet Union. Most still displayed the glorious reign of the Soviets, blind dedication to the State and its leaders and happy workers all round.

These displays simply have to change.

Our first stop outside Tashkent was Bukhara: a multi-faceted city referred to as a "city museum", "wise", "blessed", "learned", "refined", the most popular being "*Bukhoro i Shariff*" meaning "Noble Bukhara". True to its name, this city is regarded as the second most holy city for Muslims. It is situated on the outskirts of the Kyzyl-Kum Desert meaning "red sand" and is therefore very dry and very dusty. This region is known for its contaminated water – NOBODY drinks it!!! In fact the water is so salty, the more tea you drink, the thirstier you get – how's that for being weird? There are no cold drinks in sight so it is tea, tea and more tea...we can only dream about Coca Cola!

Bukhara has a population of 250 000, the majority being Tajik and a minority of 4 500 Bukharan Jews who have been here since 600 AD. There are many beautiful blue-domed mosques decorated with colourful mosaic tiles in crisp greens, blues and whites. It is said that the large, shiny, blue domes were used as landmarks for camel caravans through the desert, the sun reflecting on them during the day and a fire lit on top of them at night. Near the mosques and *madrassas* (Islamic schools) are large pools, possibly used for religious cleansing. They provide a welcome cooling effect on hot days in the city. A prominent structure is the minaret built in 1100, the *Minora Kolon* (which literally means "small tower"). This was the tallest building of the ancient world. Most of the religious buildings are still being used as mosques and Islamic schools, but some of them have kept their Soviet obligations as shops selling fabrics and horrible Soviet-made junk.

Although only the older Uzbeks wear traditional outfits: brightly striped prayer coats that would make Joseph's dream coat look dull and boring, long grey beards, black rubber Aladdin-shoes with pointed toes and black and white caps called "*Dupas*" – all Uzbeks boast a rich traditional Uzbek culture with the exception of a few Russified Uzbeks who cannot even speak the national language.

There is more than enough food and no violence – contrary to popular belief!

I will tell you more in my next letter.

Felicity and Michael

Dear Friends,

We are currently living with an Uzbek family in Bukhara. Karim is a paediatrician and the rector of the local medical college, Farida is an anaesthetist at the polyclinic and they have two children: Guli (16) and Laziz (12). Unlike most Uzbek families, they have everything that opens and shuts, including a microwave oven, colour-screen computer (used only for computer games) three colour TV's, video players, and a gamut of techno-gadgets neither they nor I know how to use. Despite these Western aids, we have tried to immerse ourselves into this very new and very different Uzbek culture. So much for a flat-roofed hut with clay walls with no electricity or running water – naturally our disappointment wasn't great when we didn't find what we had anticipated!!!!

We have learned to eat and enjoy most of the Uzbek food that has been put before us. By the way, there is plenty of it. We eat a lot of bread (round, flat loaves) baked in traditional clay ovens outside, very feisty-tasting mutton, from very mature sheep, and fruit, mainly grapes, melons, apples and pomegranates. The family has their own cow so all dairy products are home-made and VERY fresh. They also have their own chickens and sheep. It is very difficult to eat and animal you previously knew, even if it was only by sight. *Pilaf* (also known as *osh* in this part of the world), a rice dish made with meat and carrots, is very popular and is eaten every Thursday. Fatty meat and oil seem to be a staple, so we fear for our hearts (and our outward composition). Fat that we would normally trim, is what Uzbeks seem to enjoy most. Uzbeks believe that the copious amounts of hot green tea drunk during and after a meal, melts down and dissolves all the fat and therefore there is no fear of cholesterol...pity the rest of the world doesn't know about this yet. I hope it works for us....

Shopping is nothing we've ever experienced before. The phrase "shop 'til you drop" has taken on a whole new dimension. Because of the collapse of the Soviet Union, there is nothing left to buy. Uzbekistan is not in the position to produce her own goods and importing goods is forbidden by the Government – with the result, there is nothing to buy. The Uzbeks however, being very keen businessmen, are not hampered by this at all. Shelves are filled with one or two products. The local grocery store, for example, has two products: petroleum jelly and fax rolls. The shop is jam-packed with these two items. It's weird having more than enough money and not being able to spend it, except of course, if I want to stock up on fax rolls or petroleum jelly!

Our toilet paper story is a gem: where do you think you would buy toilet paper? No, not the supermarket silly, the stationery shop – along with all other paper products. Well, after we were desperate for toilet paper, our host decided to help us solve the toilet-paper-shortage problem by driving us to a village where he knew the mayor. You see, knowing someone of stature in a town opens doors for all kinds of miracles… even the door to the stationery shop that sells scarce toilet paper. We left there with the shop's entire stock – we can now wipe our bums for the next 10 years!!!! Mind you, the particular type of toilet paper is so coarse, one would probably use it so sparingly, it might even last forever!

Funny, isn't it? This is how people live. They have cellars underneath their houses and they stock-pile everything, in fear of a product running out. Our family has a stock of more than 50 teapots, in preparation for their son's wedding – and he is only 12!!!!

Shopping in the market is an entirely different experience. The rows and rows of colourful fruit, vegetables and nuts are a feast for the eye. A true Asian experience: tasting, haggling weighing, paying and carrying oneself to death.

Learning Uzbek is as difficult as learning any new language, but we are mastering some catch phrases which get us in and out of trouble. Some useful phrases are: "how much is this", "it must be cheaper" and, "no thank you, I already have enough toilet paper, but would you like to buy some from me?" have proven to be quite useful.

I have started teaching English at the language centre – evening classes for adult professionals and businessmen. I am also waiting for the university students to return from picking cotton for the collective farms in the area. Every year, at harvest time, all students in the country are mobilized to hand-pick cotton – cotton is the country's "white gold" and if it is picked by hand, it fetches a better price.

Receiving my monthly salary has also been a cultural experience. The 4000 Rubles that we earn is delivered in five and ten Ruble notes. I need a large bag to carry my salary home each time I am paid – and then there's nothing to spend all this money on!!!

It is true that "red tape" originated in the Soviet Union. We have been issued with loads of identity cards and letters, we have to sign books and registers before we can receive anything and…. we even had to have an AIDS test the other day!!!! Control is the name of the game.

Most people call themselves Muslims even though they are not very committed to practicing their faith. Despite Bukhara's fame as a prominent Islamic centre, Communism prescribed atheism until "*perestroika*" (the revolution in 1988). For the last four years people have returned to their traditional Muslim roots even though most of them know very little about their faith. Many "Islamic" beliefs here seem to be a mixture of folklore and culture – things like believing that God will bless you with a child if you cut up a potato, bury it under a tree under the light of a full moon and wait…

I'm off to bury my "eye of newt"….

Until next time,

Felicity and Michael

10 January 1993

Dear Friends,

Greetings from Tashkent. Yes, we have moved from Bukhara to Tashkent, the capital city of Uzbekistan, after being deemed to know the language and culture well-enough to "survive". What on earth does "survive" mean when "PECTOPAH" is still not a "restaurant"? My library skills are being used to good effect, with the arrival of 30 000 English books which I am required to transform into a user-friendly, computerized, western-style library for Uzbeks who are able to read English (and also the curious ones who can't). English books are rare items in Uzbekistan, so this library will be an oasis in the desert, literally speaking.

Michael and I live in a two-bedroomed, furnished flat in the city. The description of the décor in this flat is far beyond words. Some adjectives that come to mind are: kitsch, tacky, tasteless, stuck-in-the-sixties – with its shocking pink marbled wallpaper in the kitchen and the same style wallpaper in turquoise in the bathroom – even on the ceiling!! We managed to dispose of the heavy gold curtains that covered the windows and doors. We still have not worked out why there is sound-proof padding on the walls in the entrance hall. Perhaps time will reveal all. Nevertheless, it is comfortable and it's home.

Not living with a local family has changed our concept of living in this country: standing in line, bucket in hand, for milk or cream; watching the butcher chop the carcass of an animal up with an axe (there are no electric saws) with the head of a cow on the counter eyeballing every move (meat can be bought privately from car boots outside the market); apparently it is fresher as long as it's not road-kill. Pushing, shoving, haggling; buying eggs in plastic bags; buying chickens, plucked or un-plucked, with heads and feet attached (commonly known as "walkie-talkies" in Africa….) The average "pop in to the store to buy a few things" could amount to six hours of shopping – and then everything needs to be carried home, via the metro! No, I'm not complaining. At least I know I won't have to do this forever.

As you can imagine, Christmas and New Year was celebrated with a difference. Everything that belongs to Christmas was evident: snow, trees, decorations (minus angels and a manger), Santa, gifts, but no Christmas carols playing in the background of every shop and shopping centre or nauseating Christmas sales, let alone the endless Christmas advertising on radio and television. All these "Christmas icons" marked the celebration of New Year. Christmas came and went as a non-event - 25 December was a normal working day. New Year, however, is welcomed with each family at home, eating a meal together.

We celebrated New Year with our "adopted" family in Bukhara. Family and friends visit one another in their homes but make sure they are home in time for their meal at midnight, after which neighbours, family and friends come around with good wishes for the coming year. It is imperative that the table is laden with food – the more food, the more prosperous the coming year will be. Can you imagine STARTING to eat a feast at MIDNIGHT???? Every person around the table, starting with the oldest male, gets to toast the new year with locally-made champagne (I know it's meant to be called "sparkling wine" but not in this neck of the woods) moving on to vodka – an age-old Russian tradition that most people here just can't seem to shake off, even though they are Muslims. As the party gets rougher, the toasts get more philosophical and longer, until the sun starts to rise, the eyelids start to droop and the brain can no longer make any sense of anything.

Winter is well and truly here with snow, ice and cold. Fortunately all the homes are well-heated. Hats, coats, scarves and boots are the order of the day. Michael looks like a member of the Russian "Mafia" with his big

black coat; karakul fur hat and beard.
   A prosperous New Year to you all,

   Felicity and Michael

Dear Friends,

Just when you thought we might have been shipped off to Siberia – greetings from Uzbekistan. Winter is finally drawing to a close, and with its ending we are more than pleased to say goodbye to cabbage, beetroot and carrots. We anxiously await the arrival of Spring and its new culinary delights. Yes, we have finally discovered a weight-loss programme that does work!!!!!

For relaxation we occasionally indulge in a ballet or an opera, a heavily state-subsidized luxury which will probably soon come to an end. A ticket costs less than 50 cents. Unfortunately only about 25 people attend the performances which is a pity, because a lot of work is involved, and the standard is reasonable. The Opera and Ballet Theatre in Tashkent was built in the 1940's by the Japanese prisoners of war. It is obvious that the Japanese captured in the USSR were only used for their labour because the building is in the style of the Bolshoi Theatre in Moscow. Very opulent, very Russian. The stucco moulding inside is like the icing on a wedding cake, complemented by rich maroon velvet seating and luscious navy blue velvet curtains decorated with rich gold embroidery. I personally love the private boxes on the sides of the theatre where one can sit in voluptuous couches with tiny, intricately decorated fake ivory opera glasses and watch the performance from the side. This often means seeing only half of the performance, since it was built such that only half the stage can be seen. What the hang, it is so cheap, one can see the performance from the left on the one night, and return the following night to see the right-hand-part of the performance. Such decadence!

A large portion of our time is swallowed up fighting bureaucracy. It is becoming more and more stressful to live in this country as a foreigner. Management of foreigners within the country is strictly controlled. We now need passports and a visa to catch a bus, train or plane to any city within Uzbekistan. It is said that government control is stricter than during the time of the Soviet Union, the reason being, they never had foreigners living here before so they don't quite know what to do with us.

Michael's work takes us all over the country. This sounds exotic, but it's not. Our choice of transport is bus, train or airplane. The buses are regular, but overcrowded, so one needs to get to the bus station early in order to get a seat, otherwise it is standing room only, this can be quite taxing especially if the journey is six or more hours. The trains run only at night. Apparently this was done during the Soviet era so the people (the plebs) didn't get to see the poverty (or the existence of the village people) of the rural areas. There are three different classes: 2nd class – exposed and noisy (a bit like a cattle truck with bunk beds); 1st class – a four-berth compartment with no guarantee of who one's room-mates will be – Western shoes and clothes are in great demand so you have to sleep with all your belongings tied to your body. The SV (the Russian acronym for "*Spalny Vagon*" which means "Sleeping Wagon") class, a coach formerly dedicated to Communist Party officials, which consists of a coupe with a door that locks, clean linen, embroidered curtains, lights that work, a crackly radio that cannot be switched off or turned down and a pot of hot tea served on a table covered with a white linen tablecloth (remember "some are more equal than others" – George Orwell.) The difference in cost between 2nd class and this class is about $1, and acquaintance with the right people... at the right time.

Contrary to popular belief, the airplane is not the most convenient form of transport. They are frequently delayed and very noisy, being 30-seater, turbo propelled, Russian-designed, Uzbek-made pieces of airborne metal. A comment frequently heard at the airport: "No, there is no flight today, but you are just in time for yesterday's flight which will be leaving in 30 minutes." We are however, coping with the country's transport system and it serves our needs adequately.

Michael has just finished hosting a four-day staff conference at a popular (it's popular here at least) ski resort in the Chimgan mountains. Calling it a "ski resort" might just make it sound more elaborate than it really is. The hotel comes complete with sauna, Boris the Masseur, skis, chair-lifts from the 60's, four resident KGB agents and a hotel manager with a user-friendly policy: "all problems are solved with money". One thing we did learn: if you can organize a conference in the Soviet Union, you can organize a conference anywhere.

Back to Boris the Masseur: a typical Russian sauna requires that a person is hit with a bundle of leafy branches (called a "*venik*" in Russian) from either a birch or an oak tree. It is said that this brings the blood to the surface and enhances the detoxification process. This done, body red and covered in leaf-shaped welts, I lay (covered in what used to be a white towel) eagerly awaiting my "relaxing massage". In walks Boris – the enormous, non-English-speaking, very rough, masseur who proceeds to pummel my already-aching body. "Over", "down", "quiet", "too soft?" "finish", were the only words he seemed to know. I wonder what they would do to me if they try to make me divulge any secrets Soviet-style?

"*Navrus*" (Muslim New Year) was celebrated on 21 March – a more appropriate time for New Year as it marks the beginning of Spring. For the Uzbeks it seems like a national celebration rather than a religious holiday. We experienced a colourful, eventful day with every public square and park filled with music, food, national costumes and dancing. The streets and government buildings (i.e. all the buildings) were festooned with colourful flags and inspirational slogans.

There is a traditional dish that is made during this time, called "*sumalak*". This is a porridge-like substance made of finely ground wheat sprouts. This rather lengthy ceremony takes 24 hours – attended only by women. About a week before the holiday the wheat is grown into small shoots and then ground into a pulp. This pulp is then placed into an enormous cauldron over an open fire outside, and stirred for 24 hours. The women also add stones, regarded as a vital ingredient, to the bubbling brown mixture. No-one really knows the reason for the stones: some of the more practical thinkers say that it is so that the porridge-like substance does not stick to the bottom of the pot, another reason is that they serve to make it look like there is more of the porridge-like substance in the pot, other more spiritual people that is it to bring health and good luck to those who eat the contents although I don't think anyone is expected to eat the stones... The women sit up all night, sing, dance, gossip and secretly drink the undrinkable poured from teapots. It is common for women to fill their teapots with what they call "white tea" which is code for vodka. This guarantees a raucous party, enough to put any teenage shindig to shame. In the morning the *sumalak* is left to cool, divided into bowls and distributed throughout the neighbourhood. This is supposed to contain all the nutrients required after and long, bare winter. The unmarried girls get the stones for good luck – in most cases, "good luck" means finding a husband before the age of 20.

We are also in the throes of Ramadan (a month of fasting for Muslims). We have noticed that not many people are taking part in the fast. Most have opted for a three-day fast in order to appease their conscience and Allah (who can't be paid off but apparently, can be cheated). Some even have a doctor's certificate to verify that they may not fast because of health reasons. Who is going to read that? God!!

Language study??? Yes, we are studying Uzbek, and have been since we arrived. We have now reached that stage where we THINK we can keep a simple conversation. The rewarding part is that all Uzbeks love it when we try to speak their language – for some reason they think all Europeans can speak Russian. Possibly because, to the untrained eye, Europeans look like Russians, or because no-one in this whole wide world would ever choose to learn to speak Uzbek except for me..... and that is only because I am rather nationalistic by nature and feel that by learning the mother-tongue of this nation that has been denied this for more than seventy years; I am doing my part in making a statement of nationalism and human rights. On a more practical note, when I go to the market and try to negotiate in Uzbek, I usually end up getting my produce for free, plus a cup of tea and an impromptu conversation with about fifty curious onlookers. I LOVE the attention!

Until next time,

Felicity and Michael

Dear Friends,

My, but time flies when you're having fun! In fact, so fast that Spring has been and gone since we last wrote. Spring was glorious! Everything was fresh and beautiful – the neighbourhood streets are lined with the blossoms of fruit trees and everything is just a fairyland of pink and white. We lived on fresh strawberries and cream for a month! This luxury was, however, short-lived and summer has barged in like an unwelcome guest. We have never experienced such HEAT. Michael says that it feels like his bones are being boiled. The average temperature is 45 degrees Celsius. The temperature, according to our "private thermometer" at home has managed to reach 54 degrees. We are never sure what the REAL temperature is because the weather programme on Uzbek TV does not reveal the whole truth – heat is all in the mind. Why should we know the truth, it will just make us hotter? Even the tar roads feel like marshmallows. Fortunately we have an air-conditioner, so we will survive the summer.

On the work front: Michael almost ran his legs off preparing for the staff exodus for the Summer holidays. This included buying air tickets (which is not as simple as just picking up the phone and making a booking). We need permission to leave the country, permission to take excess baggage on the plane. Who knows if anyone will be allowed to come back from their holidays…

I hope to open the library on 1 September. This is Uzbekistan's Day of Independence and this year's so-called "Day of Knowledge". This sounds like an ideal day for a library to open. "Library?" you may ask. Yes, who would have thought I would use my skills and training as a Librarian in this part of the world. I am involved with, what I call, a unique project, hosted by the University of World Languages here in Tashkent. They received a 40-foot container full of books donated by people in the United States. Boxes and boxes of books were collected by a company called "Books for the World", stuffed into a container and shipped off to the back-of-beyond. My job has been to open all the boxes, sort through the contents, making some kind of academic sense to the collection, classify them (yes, I did use the Dewey Classification System) catalogue them on computer, label them and shelve them.

I have had many young students volunteer to help me unpack the million (it seems) boxes of books. This is terrible work but they keep coming back for more – this, I have since been told (secretly by those who know) is firstly, but not most importantly, to practice their English by chatting to me but also to inform the KGB as to what books will be on the shelves in the library. Yes, to my astonishment, some of the students are paid by "others" to take careful note of what will be on the shelves once the library is open. Keep in mind, the written word was very much controlled during Soviet times. The government would decide which books were to be housed in libraries and sold in bookshops, they decided which books would be translated and used in schools. Some older English speakers hold, with tears in their eyes, copies of Shakespeare's plays in original English – they have never seen such a thing. They devour every three-year-old National Geographic and Newsweek magazines with a hunger and an interest I've never seen before. What a privilege it is to be surrounded by all the books they need….and we don't need.

There is still much work to be done before the grand opening, but we are beginning to see the light at the end of the tunnel. It's amazing how complicated the simplest things can become, like buying carpets, installing curtain rails, finding locks, duplicating keys and making curtains. Here is a small example of how frustrating it can be to get things done: to buy a carpet one needs to have a bank cheque because it costs more than 10 000 Rubles ($10); a cheque can only be obtained from the state banks;

to get a cheque, one needs a Soviet passport i.e. a willing Uzbek friend (foreigners may not get cheques and may therefore, not buy anything for more than $10); then one needs to stand in line for at least an hour to get the cheque, after an hour it is either tea-time or lunch-time and the cashier will close her counter window, which is a small hole-in-the-wall, with the horrible dirty curtain. This is rudely done in front of the next customer in the queue; after lunch one begins again; once this precious item is obtained, one then rushes to the furniture shop, cheque in hand, only to find the carpet sold because there is such a demand for carpets. The process begins again. Thank God for cash machines!!!!

If you have a book on your bedside table you haven't looked at recently, read it, it's a privilege we take for granted.

With much love,

Felicity and Michael

Dear Comrades,

Greetings from the "Former Soviet Socialist Republic of Uzbekistan" – the motto of our country is "independence, peace and co-operation": the first was given two years ago, the second we try to maintain, and the third is still an elusive concept (referring to the bureaucratic red tape we always manage to be wound up in).

Speaking of Independence, Uzbekistan's second year of Independence was celebrated on 1st September with much pomp ceremony. The main square (incidentally, it's called "Independence Square") is transformed into a giant stage, serving as a platform for thousands of children who are brought in from all the regions throughout the country to sing about the joys of living in Independent Uzbekistan. These impressive, large-scale performances are shown on gigantic screens all over the city, aired on TV, and heard through millions-of-megawatt-loudspeakers. The President attends this concert in person, with his entourage of bodyguards – the audience has to be searched and seated two hours before the festivities begin – just in case... The evening begins with his arrival and the bellowing of the National Anthem, followed by about two hours' worth of singing, dancing, military bands, marching music, colourful costumes, sound effects, lighting, and speeches all performed by the country's best – including sons and daughters of Government officials, or relatives of anyone who is someone. It ends with a million Dollar fireworks display that can be seen by all inhabitants of the city and possibly even those on the moon and Mars! The festivities are enjoyed by one and all, whether live or on TV. A bit reminiscent of the glories displayed during Soviet times.

This year's Independence Day celebrations ushered in the long-awaited opening of the *Mustaqillik* (Independence) International Library. Among the invited guests was the Minister of Higher Education of Uzbekistan, the American Ambassador, a variety of diplomats, rectors of universities and other high-brows. The Prime Minister was supposed to attend but he never turned up, but because of his assumed presence the run-down building was completely renovated and painted. It turned out to be quite an impressive occasion with me being interviewed for the Television News programme and the Uzbek version the "Breakfast Show". This momentous occasion was even reported on Radio Moscow – nothing like keeping a low profile. I am pleased that I have finally reached the end of the road. I do realize however, that this is really just the beginning. Selecting members, registering users, teaching them how to use the library, public relations, reading, and other academic-related activities will keep me and my staff extremely busy. This project has been a great success – the Uzbeks are thrilled with their new library.

It has been an interesting experience living in a fast developing country, things change daily. The government has released its control on the prices of some commodities and, as a result, things have gone crazy. Petrol (gas for Americans and benzene for Uzbeks) disappeared for a while and transportation became increasingly difficult. The streets emptied out and there were fewer and fewer cars, taxis and buses. Buying petrol became an art: our driver had to set off after midnight in search of petrol. Usually in some neighbourhoods (one had to know which ones) there would be the oddest assortment of people milling around in the streets – from small children playing games to an old lady with her sheep and cow. Our driver would slow down, make an unnoticeable-to-the-human-eye-signal with his hand and someone would suddenly jump onto the back seat of the car. This person would guide the driver to the house that was selling the petrol. The driver would drive the car into yard, close the gates, and then the black market transaction would take place – for foreign currency only.

These people desperately need some lessons in Capitalism, or do they?

The concept of supply-and-demand is fully understood and even more fully exploited. Is this another form of Capitalism perhaps?
Regards,

Felicity and Michael

Dear Comrades (we hope you are getting used to this idea)

"Africa revisited" was an unexpected, yet wonderfully refreshing time for us and of course, it's good to be back with family and friends. The warm sunny days of an African summer rescued us from the unusually long and coldest winter in Asia for 70 years. Our return to Uzbekistan reminded us of the camel traders of old – heavy laden with goods from the wealthy west. We carried everything from coconuts to fabric softener. We even managed to bring two grass doormats from Zululand which the Uzbeks wanted to hang on their walls. A snowstorm awaited us on arrival in Tashkent, everything looked so beautiful and for a brief moment, it seemed a pleasure to be back "home".

In such a fast-changing country we found out just how many things can change in three months. One radical change was the currency. We now have to work with an intermediate currency which works on a coupon system. We are in transition between the Soviet Ruble and our very own currency. Along with the change came the extreme price increases, shortages of goods and general chaos, however, things are beginning to stabilize now and we are managing to operate reasonably smoothly with nobody starving… yet. The official exchange rate is 1 600 Soum to one US Dollar and the unofficial rate is 13 000 Soum to one US Dollar. It is also possible to negotiate your own exchange rate with the bank, so things are pretty flexible at the moment. The bottom line is: everybody wants hard currency. To give you a rough estimate, we pay 13 000 Soum for one kilogram of meat. Enough about money!

We have moved from our stuck-in-the-sixties-flat! It is wonderful living in a spacious house instead of a pokey little Soviet flat, although living in a flat is far more social, mixing with the local people who always seem curious about our daily habits. We have been able to acquire a cosy little two-bedroomed house of our own. As a result of the CRAZY rent situation in Tashkent at present, we felt it would be a wiser proposition to shrug the greedy landlords off our backs and replace them with a not-so-greedy banker. Actually, our greedy banker turned out to be an old Russian-Jewish *babushka* (old lady – usually a grandmother). This is how the sale of a house works: the buyer and seller go together to the lawyer's office to prepare the deed of sale. The buyer pays half of the negotiated price and the papers are signed. Then they need to go to the registrar's office to register the house in the buyer's name. In the meantime, *Babushka* (representative of the seller) and I (representative of the buyer) wait in the house, money in hand, cash – in my hand. Once the registration is done, the buyer who in this case is Michael, phones the buyer's representative to say that all is in order. On cue, I hand the remaining 50% to *babushka* and the sale is done.

The house had been standing vacant for three years so you can imagine the state of it! Repairing and renovating presented yet another one of the many challenges of this country: painting with no paint, re-glazing with no glass, re-flooring with no wood, re-plumbing with no pipes… however, after countless trips to the hardware bazaars and markets, we managed to transform it into what we proudly call "home". Michael has proved to be quite a handyman, the most stringent test being assembling the kitchen cupboards with instructions in Russian! All the work was finished in six weeks and we have settled in now and are very happy with our situation. We have familiarised ourselves with our new neighbourhood, making new friends and finding out where the necessary shops and transport routes are.

Now that we have a bigger house we have a constant stream of guests and are being kept busy with cooking, shopping, general chores of keeping the house going and of course, entertaining. I have the luxury of a housekeeper and a chef because of all the functions we are "expected" to host in the expat community. Sasha is a skinny young man (someone once told me to never trust a thin chef), Russian and trained as a baker. He knows English but his "cooking-English" is limited, so we work out of recipe books with elaborate photographs and diagrams and an English-Russian dictionary. Given all this literature, there have been some cultural misunderstandings. An example the day I asked him to make *rusks* (very chunky, very dry, bread-like biscuits which are softened and eaten after dipping it into a hot cup of coffee) for the visiting South African Director of Coca Cola. The hand-written recipe from Aunty Joey in Nelspruit said, "roll the dough into *boerewors*-shaped rolls". Little did I realize that in different countries the concept of a sausage (*boerewors* translated) is vast and when these rusks were served, they came out as long, skinny sticks, very far from the rusks we were expecting! Russian sausages are certainly very different in shape and size from South African sausages. Sasha is responsible for delicious milk tart, crème Brule, scones, and other such wonderful things. My life has changed drastically since the arrival of Sasha, and so has my weight! Where will I find a gym?

We also indulge in the luxury of live musicians to entertain at functions, there are so many excellent musicians who are presently out of work, the choices are endless: chamber music, jazz, folk music, soloists, opera singers and more.

Off to look for a gym….

Until next time,

Felicity and Michael

Dear Fellow voters (or is it comrades???)

Congratulations to South Africa and our new government. We were overjoyed to hear that everything went off peacefully and reasonably smoothly. We regret not being in South Africa at such an exciting time of change and adjustment, mind you, we go through change and adjustment daily here where the situation seems so similar.

"We simply have to vote, but where and how?" was our dilemma as we sat here in the back-of-beyond. The matter was fortunately decided for us as we were given permission (with the status of a local) to buy tickets at the local price i.e. $100 return to Turkey for both of us (a five-hour flight). The Soviet Union has this crazy, yet convenient, system of subsidized air tickets for local people, foreigners have to pay the usual astronomically high price. So, with our cheap tickets in hand, we set off into the sunset on the ancient silk road to Istanbul... by airplane instead of camel.

We were guests of the Ambassador and his wife, enjoying genuine South African hospitality. Michael landed himself the job of being a voting official for the 24 that came to vote, some as far as northern Iraq! The voting ended with a tea party in the garden with *koeksusters* (syrupy deep fried South African sweet) *and pap and wors* (stiff porridge made of maize meal and typical South African sausage)... we trust your voting experience was as comfortable as ours!?!

Speaking of our fair land: South Africa now has official diplomatic ties with Uzbekistan as a result of the South African Ambassador in Turkey, Mr Neels Jakobs' visit to Tashkent, where he presented his credentials to the President. He also presented books to the library and yet another television presentation. It was a rather awkward seeing the old South

Africa flag flying next to the Uzbek flag outside the building a few days before its end (the new flag does look good, though). We had the pleasure of hosting the Ambassador and his wife in our home. Along with this came curious neighbours, private security officials, government security officials, a black chauffeur-driven car (including a flag in the front) and a bugged telephone. The telephone was so heavily bugged that it eventually stopped working. If we picked up the receiver, we could hear the soft ticking of the phone being tapped. Cheekily the Ambassador would say, "Goodnight Igor, we're going to sleep now so you can rest too." We sometimes have people phoning our home looking for a job at the Embassy since their visit.

Michael has officially been appointed (by none less than President Nelson Mandela) South African Honorary Consul to Uzbekistan. This involves taking care of South African interests in Uzbekistan, helping to promote South Africa, entertaining guests from South Africa (there have been some who have managed to find their way here) and sometimes attend Diplomatic functions. This is also all very exciting and interesting – a whole new world awaits us.

Our family has grown. No, I'm not pregnant – the TV isn't that boring! We have added two little kittens to our personal little family of two: "*Amandla*", a black cat and "*Sikeleli*", a grey striped cat given to me by an old Russian lady in the market on a cold Saturday morning. She asked/told me to hold the kitten while she went to "fetch" something. Well, she never returned and there I was, standing like a fool with a shivering, squealing kitten in my hand. The fruit-sellers, who had witnessed the event, using hand gestures, told me that the crazy woman never intended to return and motioned for me to go home with the kitten. I was mine.

At the same time Michael found Amandla, along with her pitch black siblings, in a shoebox at the front door of one of his friends. After dishing them out to onlookers, he was left with one little black, furry girl. So black, nothing shows except when she opens her mouth to show a furry little pink tongue. This all happened on the day Nelson Mandela was inaugurated as President and we thought it would be politically correct to name them as such, much to the amusement of the Uzbeks. I love listening to the Uzbek neighbourhood kids in the street shouting "*Amandla*" at the tops of their voices.

Apologies for the lateness of our letters - we don't use pigeons, instead we use people who leave the country and carry letters out for us, mailing them from England or elsewhere. As Tashkent isn't one of the popular tourist spots on the map, there aren't many coming or going – perhaps pigeons or runners would be quicker. Mailing letters from the post office is interesting. All letters are read and censored, unless they are part of a "book". All books will be posted and nothing will be read or censored, but letters may be censored to pieces, possibly never even sent... unless of course you know someone at the post office.

Best wishes,

Michael and Felicity, Amandla and Sikelele

Dear Friends,

While most of you (at least our friends in South Africa) have been experiencing the coldest winter in ages, we are barely making it through one of the hottest summers we've known and hopefully will ever know! Could someone please fix the hole in the ozone layer!!

As usual, summer has brought with it, mountains of different kinds of melons, tomatoes, peaches, apricots, strawberries and more piles of luscious, colourful fruit. Shopping in the market is a delight for the senses with the vendors who compete for your attention shouting for you to come over and try their fruit, the tastes of all the juicy fruits we longed for through the winter, and then deciding how much to buy and for what price. I usually come home with tons of fruit and vegetables of all shapes and sizes, some of which I have never even seen before.

We have been very industrious making jams and chutneys in preparation for the lean winter months. This is quite a social event with friends and neighbours and it gives us a chance to make new friends and practice speaking Uzbek and Russian. It also provides us with an endless supply of gifts to take to people when going to visit. There is no-way I will be eating the contents of 40 jars of jam and 30 jars of chutney, 30 jars of pickled cucumbers, tomatoes and red peppers and 20 bottles of wine (perhaps the wine). We are also trying our hand at sun-dried tomatoes, apparently the latest rage in Western cuisine (although here they have been eating them for possibly a few thousand years). By the way, the grapes come from our garden – apparently the vine is about 80 years old. Is that old for a vine? I'm not sure.

Summer is party season due to the abundance of fruit. In addition to regular parties, it is also wedding season which has proved to be a very busy time for us. Apparently it is quite prestigious to have a foreigner attend one's wedding. A foreigner at a wedding is known in Russian as a "wedding General". In the times of the Soviet Union, having a high-ranking military official meant one had contacts in the right places. This has dribbled down into Uzbek culture in the form of having anyone "different" at your wedding, including a "foreign freak". That's us.

Long, overly-embellished, flowery speeches of good wishes, lots of money, many children and happiness (in that order) are compulsory at a wedding – starting from the "wedding General", close family members, special guests moving through all who are in attendance and finishing with those who are too drunk to say anything significant but are still obliged to say something. Each toast is accompanied by a tot of vodka (Champagne for ladies). Given that there may be around 20 – 30 toasts at any given wedding means that one can easily demolish a bottle of vodka per person. Needless to say, the speeches get deeper, more philosophical and blurred as the night forges on.

In addition to the speeches, the toasts and the vodka is the dancing. While dancing was never one of our fortes, it has turned out to be quite fun – I think more fun for those who watch us. Dancing is quite important at weddings. It is believed that if one's guests dance a lot at one's wedding, they are enjoying it. So there is quite a bit of pressure in that area. The vodka and champagne (for ladies) helps move things along. Anyway, this provides us with very good opportunities to make friends, practice our meagre language skills and try out some new dance moves.

As time ticks on, Life becomes more and more comfortable in this developing democracy as various international companies try their hand at conducting business and investing money. State shops now stock (for many Dollars) the complete 'Old Spice' range of products, Procter and Gamble cleaning products, dishwashing PASTE from Turkey and the prince of all western consumer goods: Coca Cola. This giant step forward played an important role in seeing us through the summer. We have even managed to find selected Cadbury's chocolates for sale at the VIP lounge at Tashkent Airport. This must be one of the few places where we can say that LIFE IS GETTING BETTER! We have come to this realization since we were given access to BBC TV. Not many can say, like us, that we know how pleasant it can be, not knowing what goes on in the rest of the world.

We have bought a locally made "Moskvich" – not a household name in your neck of the woods I gather. It is not possible to buy a new car – they don't make cars here anymore and Russia is not providing any anymore. It is also unheard of to buy a foreign car, those are reserved for "those more equal" (according to George Orwell) so an old Moskvich will have to do. To begin with, we drive on the wrong side of the road (that being the right-hand-side). While watching for the usual traffic, one also has to look out for hundreds of potholes, uncovered manholes, pedestrians, people desperately hailing taxis, trams, trolleybuses, bicycles, *militzia* men (police) who frequently stop the traffic (mostly for a lift) and the never-ending tramlines that criss-cross all over the city – it's a zoo!! However, a second class ride in a car will always beat an overcrowded tram ride, especially in the summer.

For the third time since we've been here the money has changed – apparently this new money is here to stay. The new money is called 'Soum' and trades at 19:1 Dollar at the bank and 17:1 Dollar on the black market. At least our fight against inflation seems realistic. The old money bowed out at 30 000:1 Dollar so you can appreciate how we need to adapt: good for locals, very bad for foreigners. The money changed overnight without warning or opportunity to change it. At midnight, the money that people had not spent was strewn in the streets in protest. I collected it and restocked my Monopoly set. Where and how will they get new money? Rumour has it that people will be paid in "goods" for example, those who work at the glass factory will be paid in glasses and glass dishes; they will have to barter with those who work at the tomato canning factory who will then trade with those who work at the shoe factory. I sit back and wait to see what will happen. Luckily I have my jars of jam and pickles and some leftover sausage-shaped rusks that will see me through for a while.

I have become involved with the stylistic editing of the 'Uzbekistan Airways In-flight Magazine' and will help with the compilation of an English recipe book of Uzbek dishes – tried and tested! Uzbek food is not the greatest tasting cuisine consisting primarily of meat, rice, carrots and covered in freshly chopped dill. So, everything, in a nutshell, tastes like freshly chopped dill.

How are Amandla and Sikelele (our cats)? They are bounding with energy. We keep our meagre stock of *biltong* (South African slated, dried meat) with our letters – Sikelele found it and ate the biltong as well as the letters! So if we haven't replied to any of your letters you know the reason. Amandla, while romping on the floor, ran into my cello causing it to fall into pieces on the floor. If these are cats, then what's it like to have kids?!

Let's see if we can get this instrument whole again...,

Until next time.

Michael and Felicity

Dear Friends,

On the political front: we have recently had a referendum: "yes-votes" in the "yes" box and "no-votes" in the "no box" under the eagle eyes of very interested voting co-ordinators. This democratic exercise was to see whether the majority of the people wanted President Karimov to continue as President of Uzbekistan until 2000. The overwhelming 99,6% majority means that we will not be having an election next year – just as well, it seems there is much to be learned about democracy yet. To illustrate his confidence, the following was printed in the programme of the "International Tennis Tournament" held in Tashkent a week BEFORE the elections: "The people of Uzbekistan overwhelmingly voted in favour of President Karimov…."

March has been a time of a variety of national and international holidays. We began with *Ramadan*, a Muslim month of fasting from sunrise to sunset. Commitment to the Islamic faith is much more noticeable now as people are finding their religious roots. We noticed that many more people took part this year than last; people are becoming more aware of their Islamic roots. The mosques are frequently attended, some universities have introduced prayer rooms and many schools have introduced the teachings of Islam in to their curriculum. During the month of fasting, people are in terrible moods during the day because they are hungry so shopping in the market, chatting to the neighbours or simply catching a taxi can be quite traumatic. It has been recorded that during the month of *Ramadan* more food is consumed than any month of the year. Families rise at 4.00am to prepare and eat breakfast to stand them in good stead until the rush home at sunset for their next feast. Nothing much is achieved between these two meals.

We celebrated "International Women's Day" on 8th March. We had never heard of this holiday until we arrived here (usually anything that is Soviet is regarded as "international"). All this means is a day off work, flowers, long sentimental speeches wishing all the women of the world a good life (if only the men displayed similar sentiments for the other 364 days of the year), and men cooking dinner and washing up for their wives – something they justly deserve because they work so incredibly hard here.

Navrus, Muslim New Year, seemed to be celebrated with less government induced pomp and ceremony than the last one. Most families stayed at home working in their gardens, watching TV or visiting friends and family – a definite Western trend they seem to be adopting!

We were happy to have Michael's mother visit us for three weeks. She ended up having quite a challenging stay – no baggage (or *biltong*) arrived. Have you ever had a three-week holiday in the middle of nowhere with just one set of clothes!!!?? Apparently her suitcase went to India! It was delivered to our house the day after she left.

We had the joy of experiencing a breath of fresh air that was somewhat short-lived – the saga of the supermarket: a British supermarket, TESCOS (likened to Spar) opened here in Tashkent. It was wonderful! We were able to buy anything we needed, anything we wanted, and anything we craved for – like Lyle's Golden Syrup, baked beans, cornflakes, toothpaste, soft toilet paper… and then it closed, and we realized to our horror, that we should have bought at least twenty of each item. More than a month passed, we passed the shop frequently, wishing for those doors to open once again…they did!!! But alas, there was nothing to buy. All that was left was a shop with, not empty shelves, but shelves jam packed with petroleum jelly, denture cleaner and fax rolls.

As the saying goes: "All good things come to an end". Our supply of Coca Cola has also dried up because apparently there are no more bottle tops!!???

The International Community is experiencing steady growth and the ex-patriot community expands as a tremendous number of foreigners flood into the city to open businesses, embassies, etc. We wish them luck in their ventures… as long as they bring back the Lyle's Golden Syrup and the soft toilet paper!

Until next time,

Bye!

Michael and Felicity

Greetings from Uzbekistan!

We have returned from Sunny South Africa – or is it more politically correct to say "The New Rainbow Nation"? South Africa has changed in many ways and we found ourselves having to work our way through yet another cultural barrier, that of the New South Africa. We still have much to learn. There is an Uzbek saying: "The first day a guest is like gold, the second like silver and the third like MUD!" Well, your muddy guests thank you for you wonderful hospitality.

Autumn has transformed the city into a mass of beautiful rich colours. We have found though, that Autumn brings along the endless task of sweeping up leaves and finding places to dump them. There is no rubbish collection facility, so we sneak around at night finding suitable dumping spots - yet another new challenge. Many people choose to burn their leaves which results in a constant smoky haze over the city. I am not sure why we can't leave the leaves on the ground… I wouldn't dare, this house is under careful watch, our neighbours monitor every move we make…

Life, as usual, has been filled with an assortment of activities.

"Victory Day of the Great Patriotic War" was commemorated with excessive preparation and much celebration. The cities were virtually "washed and painted". The streets were painted black to make them look new, and the browning winter grass was painted green on the parade grounds! Who knows, perhaps the soldiers were also painted….? This concept is not unusual. Apparently the Russian leader of the Crimean Campaign, Gregory Potemkin, tried to impress the Empress of Russia at the time (1897), Catherine II, by ordering fake villages to be built so that she could see how prosperous Russia was as she passed through them. Today a "Potemkin Village" is referred to as something fake, something that is fabricated purely to make someone think that something is better than it really is. I must say, if it worked for the Empress then it worked for me. I was greatly impressed (and shocked) by the endless processions of soldiers and displays of military strength and fervour in the form of artillery and weapons were the order of the day, with speeches and medals all round. The government was so generous to the war veterans they gave them long-awaited telephone lines as a gesture of appreciation. These existing lines were taken away from the foreigners (so we now have no phone!!!).

We have had our fair share of excitement of late. Prince Charles visited Tashkent at the beginning of the month. For all you closet royalists, yes, we did meet him and speak to him. He came to plant a tree in the British Embassy garden. The tree was for Remembrance Day, in memory of fallen British soldiers all over the world. Quite a tired and bored looking man. The exciting part was that the Catering Business that I started with some local ladies catered for one of his functions. What a nerve-wrecking yet exciting experience. We had to make bite-sized snacks. Prince Charles had an official royal "taster" who checked and tasted all the food we planned to serve. Needless to say, Prince Charles didn't eat a crumb of it.

Michael has had a very stressful time with two sudden deaths occurring unexpectedly, one of them a very good American friend of ours. What to do? Well, this was yet another first. Did you know that the US Embassy keeps a coffin at their embassy in almost every city? Well, after mountains of red tape, the bodies were finally shipped home and dealt with in a way that we are more accustomed to.

Bruce, a good friend who came to Uzbekistan with us three years ago, unexpectedly passed away at the age of 36, in Bukhara. This was a tremendous shock for us all and, though there are many questions around his death, this incident made a tremendous impact on people's lives. He was an English teacher in Bukhara and, out of respect the local people, mostly his students and fellow teachers from the University, hosted a very touching memorial service in his honour:

These are excerpts from an article that was written about the funeral in an English newspaper:

"An elderly couple came with their children to pay their respects. The father had grey hair and wore a *dupa* (an Uzbek hat). They did not know English and they simply sat on the couch and cried. I had never seen an older Uzbek man cry before. He spoke about how Bruce had often come to their village to visit, he travelled long hours on buses just to see them. They were deeply touched by Bruce's love."

"A student of Bruce's and her father came to the house. The father had a very thick black beard and was sobbing very deeply, as much as anyone I had seen. He was a *Mullah* (head of a mosque) from a village outside Bukhara. Bruce had visited him often and they discussed Life's philosophies and the deeper meaning of Life. They said how much he spoke of his life and his beliefs. He was one of this man's best friends. He said that he loved Bruce as much as anyone, Bruce impacted his life like no one ever had."

As Christmas draws nearer we take this opportunity to wish you the very best for the Christmas season: peace, joy and everything else that goes with such a special time.

Merry Christmas!

Michael and Felicity

Dear Friends,

Winter is here! While the buzz word is "Global Warming", we have experienced nothing of the kind! The temperature has been below zero for three weeks. Our washing machine in the granny cottage outside has frozen with half-washed clothes inside! It'll have to wait until spring to complete its cycle. The clothes on the line outside are frozen stiff, like cardboard. The snow was so heavy this year, our roof nearly collapsed! During the snow-melting-time we had a steady stream of water into the middle of our dining room. We have to wait for the snow to melt before we can have it fixed. A new day… a new challenge!

Along with the frozen laundry comes the "frozen flush". Yes, the toilet in the cottage is also frozen. Thank goodness, in the main house it is warm and flushing, thanks to the Soviet policy of 'equal heating for all'… except for the grannies in their outside cottages.

Actually, I speak of the "granny cottage outside" as if it is a normal fixture of a home. This cottage, in fact, started out as a chicken coup, it was then changed into a "summer kitchen" consisting of a crude gas stove and sink with a tap, accompanied by some very dilapidated kitchen furniture. This is common in houses in this area for two reasons (that I am aware of). Firstly, the summers get so hot here, it is not very practical to heat up the rest of the house by cooking hot meals inside and therefore meals are cooked outside in the summer kitchen during the hot summer months. People also love eating outside on what they call an *aiwan* (outside porch). Here families and their guests recline late into the night under grape arbours, eating, drinking and chatting. Most gardens have a television which has been carried out side for the summer months. To cool the area, water is sprayed on the ground every few hours. Once the steam has evaporated, it can be quite cool.

Oh, and the second reason is to make jams and pickles with the summer fruits and vegetables. We turned the summer kitchen into a laundry, not knowing how much it would freeze in the winter. But back to the severe cold of the winter…

Christmas in Uzbekistan is a non-event because the 70 year of Soviet rule brought with is 70 years of atheism. This Christmas season, thanks to some expats, we were given the opportunity to sing Carols-by-candlelight. To be blatantly honest, I personally dislike rehashing the same old Christmas carols year after year but somehow, one has to bring them out of the mothballs and sing them every Christmas (at least, according to me). We even managed to sing Silent Night in Russian and Uzbek. That poor carol has really been mutilated in a million ways! Christmas at home took place in traditional style – overeating. We had some friends join us for Christmas dinner. Needless to say, it was a normal working day, makeshift turkey in the form of a few skinny chickens and squashed Christmas crackers brought back from our visit home in November. There was snow – and that made it special for us, accustomed to sweating through an African Christmas at the height of summer.

Michael celebrated his birthday in Uzbekistan with many Uzbek well-wishers, lots of food and tacky gifts. Generally gifts are given, only to be re-given. Therefore, a box of chocolates for example, should <u>not</u> be opened once it is given as a gift for two reasons: firstly, it should be given to someone else for their birthday or any other special occasion, secondly, it may had been around for so long, the chocolate may be white, chalky and possibly even accompanied by a weevil or two. For this reason, it is not recommended to open a box of chocolates or a bottle of wine in front of the guests in order to share its contents, as many cultures do, lest the giver of the gift is embarrassed no end. Nevertheless, a big party was a convenient way to catch up with friends after countless invitations to dinners, weddings and circumcision parties (more about that later).

Does "Boney-M" sound familiar to any of you? Moving away from the sensitive topics of age, taste and culture... this music group, along with Abba, is extremely popular here and they recently performed in Tashkent for crowds of fans. With our complimentary tickets in hand, we attended our first pop concert. It was like being in a time warp, the songs were at least 20 years old, but we recognized them and enjoyed them thoroughly! To our amazement, the crowd was not allowed to show any gestures of enthusiasm, if people stood up to clap, wave their arms or dance, they were immediately reprimanded by nearby policemen... just when we thought we were living in a free and happy country. Despite the restriction, fun seemed to be had by one and all.

Lots of love,

Felicity and Michael

Dear Friends,

This is still one of the only countries in the world where we can say that things improve daily. Remember the days when we couldn't find toilet paper, when there was no Coca Cola and chocolate was as scarce as hen's teeth… my, my, how things change!! We now have an Inter-Continental Hotel, a German bakery that sells sliced bread, a choice of supermarkets and photo processing services. Needless to say, prices have also "improved". One can buy a glass of Coca Cola at the Inter-Continental for $4.00, a loaf of bread for $3.00 and pork chops (in a Muslim country) for $5.00!!!! That's the expat shopping circuit – local prices remain reasonable but with a steady rise in the cost of living. People are having to hold down two, or sometimes three jobs to keep going.

The local currency's official exchange rate was 43 Soum : $1 on 1 November, the black market was 60. After the government's introduction of harsh measures to control foreign currency, the present black market rate shot up to around 110 with the official rate being 53. With the result, many foreign companies have no other choice but to leave, others are hesitating to invest their money. It appears that the economy is in decline – who knows what will happen next. As President Yeltsin said, "I only have one problem. I have 50 economists. My problem is deciding which one of them is right!"

We have a new car – the first brand new car we have ever owned!! It is a Daewoo Damas, something like a Toyota E20 that has shrunk in the wash. It looks like a tiny loaf of bread. Anyway, it is made in Uzbekistan – the South Koreans have finally managed to convince the car industry to break free from their traditional Russian-made Ladas and Volgas. They are quite cheap. It's wonderful driving around in a new car.

News Flash: Turkish Airlines has opened a direct flight Johannesburg – Istanbul – Tashkent for approximately $1000.

Michael's disaster story was his hepatitis A. He was extremely ill, laid up in bed for two months! Well, this was certainly a challenge for him and everyone in the vicinity! Our home became a hospital with drips being administered while he lay on the couch suffering the pain of badly made soviet injection needles. Blood samples were taken every third day for three weeks. Guests streamed in and out for two months bringing offerings of pumpkins, watermelons (both said to be extremely good for recovering from hepatitis) and a host of other home remedies, some of which cannot (or may not) be recorded in writing. We have a lot less of Michael around now, as he continues on his fat free diet for another six months he is managing to fit into his "Lilliputian clothes" as he calls them. The Uzbek doctor, a very good family friend, was exemplary in his treatment and advice. We are very grateful for Michael's complete recovery.

We are finding that the political situation is not as stable as it used to be. A few cracks are starting to appear in the form of increased dissatisfaction over the economic situation and much more religious activity on the Islamic front. It is still safe to live here, although many foreign investors have pulled out because of the tight economic laws.

Despite the tight economic laws, some things are loosening up. Michael was interviewed live for 30 minutes on the country's first private radio station. He was the first diplomat to be interviewed live. Most radios have to submit their programme notes for censorship at least two weeks in advance – even the news! This is quite a milestone.

With such a long winter coming to an end, our time here will come to an end in June.

It's time to leave this world of firsts. This unique transition from the restrictions of a Soviet mentality to the Capitalistic free world of "Democracy" will never be re-lived and I feel privileged to have been of the road that many, who did not even want this, have been made to walk on. It has been a few years since Communism collapsed, and many people still long for the "security" and steadfastness of Mother Russia. Most did not want independence – it was thrust on them. No blood was spilt, no-one fought for the Independence that they now have. It has given me reason to think: what exactly is democracy? I leave with a heavy heart; heavy suitcases full of souvenirs; and a wealth of experience.

Watch this space for our next stop....

Felicity and Michael

Maputo, Mozambique

10 March 2000

Dear Friends,

Our next port of call: Maputo, Mozambique. With my father struggling with his fight against cancer, Maputo serves as a wonderfully close posting, only a 90-minute drive away from "home", the place where I was born and where my family still stays. I have ended up with a wonderful posting at Maputo International School, an eclectic mix of expats and local Mozambican children, most of whom had lived abroad as children of diplomats. I had my job interview (and got the job!!!) while on holiday in India. My answers to the Director's questions were screamed down a crackling telephone line, originating in a tiny, smelly, noisy, hot and steamy telephone booth somewhere on the side of the road between Delhi and Agra.

Our third-floor apartment has a partial view of the sea, a full view of our neighbour who insists on doing his morning exercises and ablutions on the roof of his apartment every morning, and the President's house on the other side. Between the guards, the stray dogs and cats, and the peacocks from the gardens of the President's residence, walking around our apartment building, we feel perfectly safe. Life in Maputo is glorious: lots of sun, sand, sea, seafood, and social events. We have bought a zooty maroon Rav 4X4 which I love driving. I belong to a madrigal-singing choir directed by the eccentric Director of the British Council, and I go to Tai Chi classes twice a week run by a crazy Brazilian mercenary (I think).

Work is such fun, it is almost non-existent. Music classes are spent in the shade of the African flame trees dotted around the school yard, drumming with teenagers for part of the school day while another small part is singing songs like "Ten fat sausages sizzling in the Pan" with Grade one's and two's. I share the Music Department with a larger-than-life, extroverted pianist and jazz singer called Aderito who sings in clubs in the evenings until five or six in the morning and then comes to school to sing songs with toddlers. Such is life in Mozambique.

A National law (or so it seems) is that all schools and activities related to schools should finish at midday on a Friday after which everyone makes their way to their weekend activities: some to the sandy white beaches north of Maputo, some to the wild animal reserves, some to the islands to laze about and catch fish and some to the nearest town in South Africa where shopping, movies, doctor visits and other exciting things can be done. This is most often my route – to spend time with my Dad.

The bane of every music teacher's life is the musical extravaganza that is expected to be produced every year to show off the talents of the "little ones". Actually, for those of you who are parents or grandparents, if the truth be told, it is really for YOU to show off your little ones. As for most teachers at any school, this means a nightmare from beginning to end. The theme for this year is: "Music through the decades". Each grade level was given a decade to depict on stage. Here is a small window through which we can see one of the many final dress rehearsals before the show:

Maputo International School's Annual Musical Extravaganza

I was, thrown into the deep end. This is something of what the teachers had to say, at the 11th hour, managing a stage full of wriggling kids:

Willem: "Aderito is not feeling well and he might not be able to be here for the annual musical production. Could you fill in for us if necessary?"

Anna *to a student*…. "Where's your bottle of whiskey? Run to the class and get your whiskey!!!!!"

Willem: "Remember, you are stupid, idiotic dwarfs who know nothing – now do it!"

"You don't really love him, this is acting, now love him on the stage!!!"

Shiela: "Play, Aderito, Play!!" *(poke, poke on the shoulder)*

"What!"

"Anything, that bikini song. Play! Now!"

Jane: "Sounds a bit tinny, doesn't it?"

"They just started without me! They don't seem to need me."

"I think they've had enough hula-hoop-music. Switch off the tape."

Felicity: Wait, It looks like they're enjoying themselves.

"Stop them, I think their tummies are empty."

Linda: *(Hands in the air, to a student)* "Tell him!!!!! He can do it; we have gone through it 100 times!!! Now on your own: NO MORE WAR. That's all you have to say… three little words!!!"

"Come on; twist, like you're putting out a cigarette on the floor."

Seru: "Bring out the zombies"

"Aderito, BIG PROBLEM, no smoke!"

Peter: not a word. (bites bottom lip) not a word (bites bottom lip) not a word (bites bottom lip). AMAZING!!!!!!

Albert: *(Friday night)* "Ladies and Gentlemen, may I present to you third grade… I mean fourth grade."

(Saturday night) "Ladies and Gentlemen, may I present to you third grade, I mean fourth grade.

"Could you just play Freddie Mercury's Bohemian Rhapsody on the piano please…?"

Sister Albert, what are you teaching those Backstreet Boys?… Nudge nudge, wink wink, you know what I mean. What else do you expect from kids who have to take cues from a male nun!?!

Well done to all of you, it was a fantastic performance and it was a privilege to get a small insight into "life in elementary school".

Operation Art Safari

Another very interesting aspect of Maputo is that apparently it is has one of the world's most concentrated collection of Art Deco buildings, even though some of them have been shot to ribbons by the war between the Renamo and Frelimo in the 1970s. Here is a description of a two-day art tour through this extremely interesting, possibly forgotten city:

On a random Saturday morning in Maputo we are met by our guides Jane and Walter, two very knowledgeable specialists of the art world in Mozambique. On arrival we lunch at Sophia's, a very noisy, busy, but spirited restaurant serving the most delicious prawns, calamari, fresh bread rolls and a cold glass of "Dosh EM", a locally brewed beer.

Lunch done, our guides take us down a maze of red sand roads to the foundation of much of the art in Mozambique – the Chissano Gallery, in Matola, a region outside Maputo. As we pile out of our car, we are enveloped by the strains of a fusion of African jazz, township and Reggae music, coming from the *Baraccos*, a neighbourhood watering hole for men. We are cordially met by Pasquale, student and curator of the gallery. The house and garden are immaculate; it's almost as if he was waiting for the arrival of Alberto Chissano himself.

From the outset it is evident that Chissano was part of the revolution. The spirit of struggle, both human and political, and the conflict between Frelimo and Renamo, The disparities between the Frelimo and the Colonialists, rich and poor, haves and have-nots permeate every space of Chissano's house. We move through each stage of his artistic development, surrounded by totem-pole-like carvings of desperate humans crushed under clumsy, uncaring feet, frantic faces of despair trying to protect their skinny bodies from destruction, with fat, healthy and happy looking figures perched victoriously at the top, oblivious of what despair lies beneath.

As we walk through, Walter explains how Chissano bought a work from each of his students, as a representation of his mentorship. These works line the stairway to the next floor. Other prominent Mozambican artists such as Malangatana, Lopez, Muhlanga, Viktor Souza, Tinga, and others make their way through the multitude of wooden sculptures. As we leave this emotionally loaded space, we are taken through the garden to two galleries, one which displays the works of local Mozambican contemporary artists and another, built around the ceremonial family tree - both rich with representations of art in this country.

Emotionally taxed and deeply pensive, we take leave of Pasquale and a very much "alive" Chissano who lies peacefully in his grave in the shade of the front garden of his house.

Walter, a 5th year architecture student, is very excited to show us the *Se Grado Familia* Church safely tucked away, deep in Matola. This Pancho Guedes designed building is our next stop. His excitement is contagious as he explains how the Latin cross is used repetitively as a motif throughout both the exterior and interior of the structure: the free-standing bell tower, the cornices, the pedestals, podiums, even the metal plate lights repeat the shape of the Latin cross he has chosen to represent in his creation. The entire building, clearly displaying his tell-tale asymmetry, is styled on the idea of a ship's hull, replacing the dragons that would appear on the bow, with crosses. This is truly a rare find, a perfect sample of Guedes' work and an equally perfect example of Art Deco architecture. We leave this gem of the 50s safely hidden in the shade of the African flame trees that surround it, both overwhelmed and amazed. Is there anything that can beat this?

The Cardoso Hotel will be our home for the night. We are welcomed by the red skies of a typical African sunset. Jane, our guide tells us that the iconic white Art Deco hotel of the 1920s was bought from a Portuguese businessman by an Italian couple in 1932. After the death of her husband, Aida Sorgentini continued to run the hotel, living in a lavish penthouse until she died not too long ago after seeing the hotel pass through WW2, the Mozambican civil war, in addition to the countless interesting guests meeting to discuss various "political issues" including some of the details of the peace agreement between Renamo and Frelimo in 1991.

After a seafood dinner at the Yacht Club and music at the Old Railway Station, we fall into our beds as we try to rest our weary minds, still buzzing with the gamut of emotions stirred by Chissano's poignant messages to the world.

The next day, Sunday, we embark on our walking tour through Maputo's unspoiled neighbourhoods. We pass the Museum of Natural History, an ornamented white Manuelian-style building which used to be a school in the early 1900s. The barley twisted decorations and the cross-on-top-of-the-armillary-sphere is an obvious indication of Manuel I of Portugal's style. We pass many Portuguese-style homes decorated with intricate *Azulajo* tile facades, a crisp white Arabic-style home which now houses the Museum of Geology, and numerous Art Deco houses and flats from the 1930s onwards. The Portuguese Embassy, a multi-storey building painted in what is sarcastically known as "Colonial Pink", towers over the city while the Vila Algarve stands partly demolished, a reminder of the not too distant past of the country.

Pancho Guedes' first work (1951) is known by the people of Maputo as the "House of the Dragon" because of its mosaic of three dragons made of natural stone at the entrance of the building. He plays with various levels of function, form and fun, incorporating ergonomic features such as vertical, horizontal and zigzagged louvers made of solid concrete, effectively managing light and temperature. The rounded balconies preclude this signature used in some of his other designs. The Greek Orthodox Church, not too far from the Guedes' dragon building, is a complete contrast, with its Basilica domes with arched windows, Italian

Cross and bell tower. The inside is heavily and very colourfully decorated with scenes from the Apocalypse.

Before venturing on to the second part of our tour, we stop briefly for coffee and pastries at a nearby sidewalk café filled with Sunday-morning-newspaper-readers. Delicious!

Raquel from Tilandia welcomes us to her Art/Flower shop. This true gem is filled with a mix of works by contemporary Mozambican artists such as Idasse, Malangatana, Mucavele, Renata and many more. A sculpture in the form of a chair made from recycled weapons by Goncalo Mabunda draws attention. "It is a result of an initiative implemented by the religious representatives in Mozambique to change weapons into art", explains Walter. Apparently there is a chair in the Vatican made by Mozambican artist Huberto under this initiative. The unique combination of flowers and art is the perfect place to sit and contemplate the messages and beauty conveyed by the artists of Mozambique.

On to Nucleo De Artes, right in one of the best-known Art Deco neighbourhoods of Maputo which consists of a formal gallery of contemporary artists in a beautifully restored house, a shady garden dotted with workbenches and easels used by a variety of artists, a large covered space serving as a communal studio for famous and upcoming artists alike. The space exudes creative thought, inspiration and artistic energy as we walk through works in progress on easels, works "hanging out to dry" and works stacked against each other waiting to be recognized, exhibited and hopefully sold. Famous artist Stevao Mucavele is spending his afternoon there painting in the shade of a typical Mozambican garden. He tells us how this association of artists serves as an inspiration to young artists from the area. The influence of artists such as Chissano and Malangatana is fused with the new life that pours out of the contemporary works that are being birthed.

The last stop of our journey is the National Art Gallery; a fine full-stop to mark the end of a journey of, not only political and social statements, but also evidence that the blood of the fathers of contemporary art in Mozambique runs deep. This summary of art in the country wraps up the vibrant and energetic styles, colours and techniques used by the artists of this country.

Our ride home takes us through Maputo's Independence square which is straddled by three distinct architectural styles: the Town Hall of the Colonial era, the Manuelian Cathedral and the brand new office building designed by the famous, contemporary architect, Jose Forjaz.

This sensory feast ends with a meal at Costa Do Sol, a famous seafood restaurant launched in the 1930s, overlooking the Indian Ocean from its black-and-white-tiled wrap-around balcony. Almost as if planned, parked outside is a fabulous relic from the 50s – a long, sleek, shiny, open-top red Cuban Classic car with the most impressive shiny chrome finishes. It felt like we entered a movie scene of a Cuban gangster movie set in the 50s. A table buckling under the fresh fish, prawns, mussels, crayfish and calamari, a cold glass of locally made beer, the music of some live Afro-fusion jazz sounding in the background, the cool breeze blowing from the ocean and a clear African sky seems the perfect way to end this day – the tranquil stars and slipper-moon of the Mozambican sky places a final touch to the tapestry of colour my eyes have feasted on the past two days. All I can wish for is more of the same.

Felicity and Michael

Sabbatical in England

Dear Friends,

Here I sit, very soon after Christmas, wishing I had written you that Christmas letter I had been planning to write for so long. I am aware that I have neglected you, not keeping you in touch with all the comings and goings of our lives, but now, as I write you this 'Nearly New Year' letter, please know that it is my intention to write more regularly. I also know, if you are anything like me, when you receive an e-mail message titled Christmas Greetings you put it away for later, and then never read it. Well, let this not be the case. Enjoy our news…

Moving to England in October was a greater challenge than I ever expected. I have always loved this country and sometimes I have secretly even wished to live here more permanently. Well, contrary to my so-called 'affinity' with the culture, being brought up with many British traditions from colonial Africa, coming to Lancaster resulted in more of a culture shock than adapting to Uzbek, Russian and Mozambican cultures! My mistake was thinking that I knew and understood the people, well I don't… they even speak a different language here in the North!! The food….. one would think that a country with so many cooking programmes on TV would know how to cook. When next in England, try what is called 'Lancaster Hotpot' - it is a white stew made with meat and FIVE wind-inducing vegetables! Can you believe that!

Michael as taken a year's sabbatical to do a Master's in International Relations and Politics at Lancaster University. We are what they call 'mature students' because, we certainly look like 'old fuddy duddies' surrounded by 19-year-olds with an array of body piercings, exposed midriffs, scraggly hair, dirty dreds and the like… when next you think you are a rather hip forty-something, visit a university campus and you will WANT to be the proverbial mutton dressed as lamb? Fortunately most people think we're staff.

We have a lovely one-bedroomed flat on campus. It is on the third floor (remember we're in Britain now) with no lift, so we get sufficient daily exercise. It has been completely renovated and refurbished, so everything is brand new. Having limited room and no garden takes getting used to. It is wonderful for Michael to be so close to his studies. He literally rolls out of bed into the lecture theatre just below our flat.

Michael loves his studies. He reads all the time and has found people that 'speak his language'. He and his fellow students can pontificate endlessly on lofty subjects such as old wars and new wars, sanctions, peace, conflict resolution, reconciliation, and more… they waffle on like the people we hate to listen to on TV. He attends lectures, gives presentations, does research in the library, writes lengthy essays and will finally write a REALLY BIG THESIS which will make him a boffin - my own personal boffin. He has certainly adapted to student life - he has not bothered to have a haircut in 3 months!!!!

I, on the other hand, am still looking for a job. England has done a very good job of keeping foreigners out of the workforce in their usual 'friendly diplomatic' manner. I have been to countless interviews with folders full of papers, certificates, references, pay slips, etc., etc., only to be sent away for yet another piece of paper. The latest hurdle is a police clearance certificate which has to be an original, current, from all the countries I have lived in in the last five years…. Naaaah, flying to Mozambique, South Africa and Uzbekistan to be fingerprinted and certified 'uncriminal' by the local police force will never happen, what do you think? They also have the wonderful 'chicken/egg' policy: I need a national Insurance number to get a job, but I can't get a national insurance number unless I have a job. As I said, they reject you in such a friendly way.

I have much to do, though. My main job is being Michael's personal typist, bibliographer, editor and private librarian. I have also made friends with my trusty vacuum cleaner which I have named Vernon - it has the cutest little face. When they delivered the vacuum cleaner to our little one-bed roomed flat I realized, 'honey, your princess days are on hold for a while.' I busy myself with household chores, cleaning, washing, ironing and cooking. I never knew that looking at a shiny kitchen floor could be so rewarding (albeit only two square meters). I must say that doing my own ironing has caused me to pack my linen and cotton clothes VERY far away. I have also come to understand why hand cream is important.

I will be doing a web-design course in the new year and continue editing and teaching English privately - these people on campus need my help - there's money to be made! There are also many societies to join and much volunteering to do. I will certainly not be bored, out of pocket perhaps, but not bored.

Then there is shopping. Lancaster is a historic town with its own castle and cathedral. It also has cobbled streets, old buildings and SHOPS. The only problem, there is no parking for our proudly purchased cherry red Volvo. English people have it very hard; firstly they have to get through the traffic in order to make it to the parking lot. Then they wait for a parking, then they have to estimate how much time they might spend shopping (I mean, who can possibly know that), then they have to have the right change to put in the parking money machine, take the ticket and stick it to the windscreen. To add to this discomfort, the shops are miles away from the parking lot, so shopping is limited to how many bags they can carry at one time. Michael will NOT go shopping with me just to carry my bags. With the result, I have to shop in instalments. Not easy!

Speaking of cars, yes, I also have to wash our car. It was quite a scary experience to operate the car wash for the first time. I can't wash the car at home; we live on the third floor! Anyway, isn't cleaning the flat enough for the time being!?!

The countryside is breathtakingly beautiful. We live on the edge of the Lake District and now have the habit of driving to a specially chosen stately home that is now a hotel, to have traditional English cream tea once a week. One sort of expects Mr Darcy, or Emma, or one of the Bronte sisters or Jemima Puddleduck to appear at any moment. The weather has been good to us. It has been cold but no too wet. Sometimes misty, which is a novelty for us. And oh, as I write this letter, it is snowing ever so slightly.

As promised, I will write more regularly so I won't waffle on for much longer. These letters should be amusing as I have chosen to be a complete foreigner in England, not even taking for granted that I understand anything of what the English do and why they do it. I will keep you updated....

In the meantime, Michael and I wish you all of the very best for this coming year. May it be one of prosperity, safety, peace and excitement.

Until next time,

Felicity and Michael

Dear Friends,

The new year is well into its second month and we have once again realized how time flies… especially when you're having as much fun as I am. My insight into English culture continues to expand and I never cease to be fascinated.

Soon after the Christmas rush of shopping, cooking and eating, the shops have what they call the 'January sales'. As well as this being a post-Christmas tradition, it is also a farce. Shop windows are clad with signs such as 'half price', 'more the 70% off selected items The big question is 'half price off what?' '70% off what?' Prices before Christmas are so high, they have to bring them down in order to get them sold at "normal prices', and in any case, no-one shops before Christmas because they know that things are going to be cheaper the day after Christmas.

People queue in front of the shops from the day before the sales start in order to get into the shop early enough to get the best bargains. Speaking of which, if there has to be a favourite British pastime, it has to be queuing. If I stand on the pavement in one place for long enough, people will start forming a queue behind me. There are queues everywhere! Even signs on the motorway that say 'queues likely'. They announce them on the radio so that when there is nothing to do on a Sunday afternoon one can get one's family together, hop into the car, buy some fish and chips down the road and rush off to the queue on the M25 for some fun. I must say, after living in Asian countries for so long, I still prefer queues to the general 'people crush' I used to experience in the bazaars, buses, and other public places.

Being true to my stubborn self, I have finally managed to get myself some jobs. Yes, I had applied to so many places, I finally had people queuing up to employ me, including a teaching agency I had applied to – without an original police clearance declaration from Uzbekistan and Mozambique!!! I must say, after teaching in English schools for a month, I must stand in awe of those who are still teaching in England. I offer them my deepest respect. For those who have left and teach elsewhere, I fully understand why you have no intention to come back and teach in England. STAY WHERE YOU ARE!!! THINGS ONLY GET WORSE!!! And you say it's because of the sunshine…

I have the fortunate job of being a supply teacher. For those who are not familiar with this concept, it is like an 'ambulance for schools'. If a school needs a teacher in a hurry, for example if the teacher phones in sick, doesn't turn up, takes time off or is just too emotionally exhausted to come to school, the school phones the teaching agency who in turn phones me. So I may get a phone call at 7am asking me to stand in for a teacher at a certain school on that day. I then jump into my car, directions in hand, arrive at the school and launch into teaching… While my speciality is music and English, I may be asked to teach geography, history or God forbid, Physical Education!!!! This was the case on my very first day as a supply teacher: I arrived at the school, files bulging with ready-prepared lessons for every possible subject a school could offer, photocopied worksheets, games, etc. only to find that the entire day would be physical education, not my forte. The first class, a room full of 13-year old boys with special needs. 'Special needs' is the latest label given to children belonging to parents who are unable to discipline their children and bring them up right. They range from attention-seeking, violent, loud, hyperactive, rude, vague, dreamy, uncoordinated, dyslexic, undisciplined beings ALL IN ONE CLASS on my first day in an English high school. The absent teacher had left me work for them - crossword puzzles!! Now give a dyslexic child a crossword puzzle and tell him to sit quietly in class and work rather than play football outside. This was the longest 50 minutes of my life.

Because of my tenacity, my sense of adventure and love for anything unusual, I continue to do this job as it takes me to places, especially in the beautiful Lake District, that I would never have visited during my time here. It also gives me the opportunity to visit a school long enough to make a mess and then leave. No commitments, no marking, no exams, and no lesson preparation. I sometimes travel to schools about 100 km away. The school I have visited most takes me right to the edge of England, and then some. It is a small remote town, with no newcomers... so you can imagine what children are produced there. The teacher I fill in for has been booked off for 3 months: nervous breakdown and depression. She is still working on getting rid of her nervous twitch. The students at the school also have all kinds of twitches. I think some of them even have six toes on one foot. All I can say is: "never live in a place where the road ends....

I almost packed it in the other day when I was called to the 8th worst school in Great Britain. Of course the agency didn't divulge that little bit of important information when they gave me my assignment. Most of the students in my class I recognized from 'crime watch' on TV. There was so much anger and aggression in the class, they threw desks around, punched the walls of the classroom... one boy twice my height and size nearly even punched me!! When I didn't let them out of the classroom on time, they just jumped out of the window. They have, what they call, teacher assistants, to assist needy students during class. The one assistant at this school was so noisy and annoying, I sent him out, not knowing that he was the assistant employed by the school. This particular school has its own 24-hour full-time policeman to break up fights and stop religious and racial rioting (and then they require a police clearance certificate from me?!?!? And as for the f*"*£$ word, it no longer sounds like a swear word to me.

I have some very good English friends and I by no means want to knock the education system, my question is: where did you go to school

78

that you came out okay? I am talking about schools in the pretty little villages we see on chocolate boxes, puzzles and biscuit tins. I cannot even begin to imagine what happens in those inner city schools we hear about so often.

I have become hard core, I say that the young people of today are too soft – conscription is the only answer! Send them to the army!

My other job is working as a receptionist at a small hotel in the Lake District. I do that job for the scenery and the beautiful drive to and from work.

Michael is still doing well at his studies. He is getting so good on the computer now; he even knows what the big 'W' stands for on his desktop... what's more, he even knows how to use it! I jest, really he is quite a wiz, he gives presentations, debates with colleagues for hours, gives advice and so on. We have crossed the first hurdle of essay-writing successfully. He is so into his studies, he never leaves home without a library book... even on a romantic weekend away. Watch out, we may even end up with a Doctor of International Relations in our midst.

The weather (another great British pass-time) has been good to us. It has not been to cold or wet.

We continue to try and get used to the food, but alas, those wind-inducing vegetables are still around. Hopefully spring will bring a welcome change of diet before we blow up. Help!

As I end this letter I would like all readers to please note that I may very well be alone regarding my views on Education in England. To any possible future employers, please note that I speak as I find, and I may find education differently in some other context, that's if I ever pluck up the courage to teach again (this serves as a disclaimer, legal or not).

Thanks to those who have visited, e-mailed and phoned us. It's great to be in touch.

Until next time,

Felicity and Michael

Dear Friends,

Another exciting account of the antics of the English is long overdue and I am sorry for not writing sooner – it's not for lack of interesting information. My jobs have been keeping me occupied and the present sunshine has kept me away from my computer.

Of the three jobs I presently have, I must say I enjoy being the receptionist in a small 40-roomed hotel in the Lake District. What I enjoy most is the drive to work and back. The work I am expected to do is not at all like anything I've been trained to do, and, the scant training that was given to me at the beginning will NEVER suffice. I must admit, I draw mostly from my experience of being a terribly fussy hotel guest myself through the years. I know what guests don't want, and to my horror, this is most of what we provide at Felicity's Faulty Towers! Believe me, I will never again complain about service, facilities, speed, price, etc. For all of you who do complain: you should know that it goes in one ear and out the other.

In addition to being the receptionist, which most people (including me at my job interview) will understand as receiving guests and making bookings, I answer the phone, take orders and serve tea or coffee in the lounge, make and tend to the fire in the fireplace (the greatest challenge is to keep it going for eight hours!), I have even prepared rooms i.e. made the beds, etc. for unexpected guests, mopped up after water pipes leaked and flooded the lounge. The hotel is deep in the Lake District, very rural, surrounded by green pastures dotted with sheep, and in spring – lambs. Now I have discovered that these cute little fluffy balls of wool are extremely noisy, so noisy sometimes even the people who come to the hotel to get away from the noise of London's traffic complain about the noise that wakes them up in the morning – bleating lambs!! Another disadvantage about pastoral living is the terrible smell, urggghhh! Manure!!! Nevertheless, it is a beautiful region and I love every minute I spend there.

The hotel is known as a 'dog friendly' hotel. Owners may bring their dogs to the hotel for the necessary break from lying in the sun, on couches and in comfy baskets. It is amazing to see the paraphernalia that guests carry in for their dogs, along with the measly amounts of human's luggage: beds, baskets, food bowls, jerseys…. There is a special room for the most eccentric of all. It has a four poster bed for human use, and a miniature four poster bed for the dog!!! One couple even ordered a chicken dinner to be brought up to the room daily – room service – for the dog!!!

Most guests are very odd (to me at least), they never cease to amuse me. In addition to the individual dog lovers who visit our hotel, we recently hosted the Annual Convention of the Bull Terriers Association. Try to imagine keeping order, answering phones and serving tea with a hotel full of crazy bull terriers dragging their even-crazier owners about on leads. We also had the Vintage Car Association, something I could quite easily deal with, except for the copious amounts of port consumed each evening resulting in very rude jokes, peals of laughter and very heavy flirting. But then there came the Leaf-blowers Convention????? You were right if you guessed that they go around fields, forests and meadows throughout the Lake District blowing the leaves to see what interesting things exist under the leaves!!!! An interesting crowd was the Hedge-Cutters Association. I kid you not – this I why I enjoy my job – I would do it for free, purely for the entertainment value.

One of the many hats I wear in the hotel is that of a barmaid, yes, a barmaid! For those of you who are not familiar with an English Country hotel's bar, it is not nearly as bad as you imagine. I managed to be an endless source of entertainment (and annoyance for some) not by dancing on the tables, but by 'pulling a pint'. The beer I poured in the beginning was shameful, usually about an inch of beer and 20 inches of foam (more correctly referred to as "the head")!!! I could see customers cringing as the glass filled in front of them. Most of them politely ordered bottles of beer if they saw me appear behind the bar. I must say that my skills have vastly improved and now I can pull a mean pint if I have to. Some of the guests however, do miss the fact that I have learnt that a tot is not half a glass; they were coming back for more gin and tonics, whiskey and waters or vodka and cokes when I was measuring… The bar was famous throughout the Lake District for a short while.

I only work two days a week, mostly on the weekend and as I said, it is definitely not for the money. In any case, it is about a 40-minute drive and the bad driving habits I have picked up from being in Uzbekistan and Mozambique have not stood me in good stead – in fact, they have cost me most of my salary each month. There are no live policemen who can be flirted with or bribed if one has gone over the speed limit. There are ugly, lifeless, strict little yellow cameras dotted along the roads. Getting a fine is quite a laborious process: first you speed, then the camera takes a photo of you, then the constabulary sends you a letter saying that the car with a certain number plate (usually mine) was speeding, then you have to admit to being the driver, then you post your admission of guilt back to the constabulary, then they send you a fine, then you pay the fine. This is all done by post and you have 28 days to complete each step. The entire process could take about 6 months all in all, except, I had sped so much, my letters and fines were piling up to such an extent that not only me, but the administration at the constabulary office was getting confused as to which had been paid and which we were still waiting for.

Anyway, I am now in big trouble and with my next offence, I will be sent to SPEED SCHOOL!!!! This will take an entire day… and I have to pay for it myself. My driving habits have been curtailed so much that I now feel I am more of a dangerous driver – as soon as I see a speed sign I slam on brakes for fear that the camera might take another picture. These cameras apparently are so vicious they can zoom right into your car and photograph you putting on lipstick, texting on your mobile or even picking your nose! Talk about control!!!!

I still manage to pluck up some courage every week to go out and teach. I can only manage three days in a row, nothing more. I have decided that there is more dignity to being a prostitute in Bangkok than there is being a teacher in England (not that I have experience of the former). All I do know is that both pay extremely well.

The most favourite British pass-time is, without a doubt, reading the newspaper. I love our local newspaper, it comes out once a week jam-packed with all kinds of interesting information about what is happening in Lancaster. My favourite page is 'Court Watch' which lists, in detail, all the crimes that have been tried in court each week. Examples of such crimes are: man steals jumbo sausage roll from street vendor, fined £4.25 (the cost of the sausage roll), another terrible incident was the theft of a pair of track suit pants that was stolen by a young girl. She was fined £10.00 because they were not sure of the value of the item. If only South African courts were forced to try such terrible felonies.

Michael is doing excellently and still loving being a student. We may have entered a lifestyle he may not be willing to leave. This is not really what I bargained for but I am happy for him. Anyway, we'll have lots of certificates to frame and hang on the wall to make him look right posh. He is in the last phase of his studies: time to write the big thesis… He spends most of his time reading, typing away on the computer, a skill he has perfected during his time here. He now knows that there is much happening beyond the big blue 'W' on the desktop. The international students in his department have also formed a great group of comrades. They discuss deep political matters, advise each other on how to go about their tasks, argue and go grocery shopping together every Friday afternoon. Who would have thought that five guys from South Africa, Namibia, Sri Lanka, Japan, Afghanistan would love to shop!!! Life is never what you expect.

On the home front, you may be wondering about my relationship with Vernon. Well, I have moved him out as I don't need him that often anymore – he lives in the corridor outside the flat. I have managed to teach the people who visit us to take their shoes off before entering, something we learnt from living in Asia and have been doing for years. My newest challenge is the smoke alarm. It is so sensitive that if I slightly burn anything is goes off. I now have to remember to cover it with a sock before I start cooking… apparently there are also fines for doing that.

Well, it is time for me to go. I have a bell-ringing lesson at the local priory – apparently it's a brilliant workout. More about that in my next letter.

Bye from both of us.

Felicity and Michael

Dear Friends,

It's about time I get down to and write some more about my favourite eccentric nation – yes, I continue to be amused by this strange and wonderful land.

We have just come out of a very gripping National Insect Week, the Royal Horticultural Society's Annual Flower Show and finally, someone has found the first hedgehog of spring in our High Alert Hedgehog Watch. Alas, we have not yet found a glow worm, we, and the presenters of Radio Cumbria, think they may becoming extinct! We do have an emergency hotline number to call as soon as we see one.

In addition to all this excitement, schools have closed for the summer, and my, what a summer it is! With record-breaking temperatures, the hottest since 1911, constant warnings not to get sunburned and rumours of an imminent drought, this Island of cold weather, rain and wind is sounding more like Africa. We now get weather reports on the radio and TV about every five minutes. Can you believe it? Farmers have even been advised to rub sunblock on their pigs! Nothing like frying your bacon ahead of time.

Drought on the Isle of Mud? As I write this there are storm clouds building up, there is not a spot on the grass on which I can walk without mud squelching though my toes. This must be the wettest drought since 1911. I'm truly getting into the swing of the British thing, look, two paragraphs devoted to the weather.

I am overjoyed that school is finished; this means no more teaching/ abuse for me. It was a kind of love-hate relationship I had with my teaching job. The more I taught the more money I made, therefore, if I was asked to substitute for a teacher for a day, even though I knew what was in store for me, it was hard for me to say no. Teaching a full day, from 9 to 3, meant I could pop over to the shoe shop at 3.30 and get myself a new pair of shoes (or sometimes something more substantial). Twenty pairs of shoes later, now that school is closed, I kind of miss it... or do I? I miss the shopping, of course!!

The end of term has also brought with it graduation season at the university. No, not for Michael yet, he is still busy completing his thesis. The Great Hall at the University is churning out graduates and their proud parents by the hundreds. Three graduation ceremonies a day – so that's what the vice-Chancellor is paid to do! I must say, the students clean up quite well, after removing their metal piercings and hiding their tattoos, they look ever so posh in their black gowns and caps.

Michael is feverishly working at finishing his dissertation. We are coming to the end of an era... only footnotes, title pages, bibliographies and binding remains. We will be leaving this sunny land at the end of August. Where to? I will reveal this in my next letter – I can assure you, not Beirut, Haifa or Damascus.

I would like to congratulate members of my family and friends who survived several weeks of being a football widow. Well done! It is so refreshing not to have to be subjected to football on the telly every night; I am beginning to wonder though, if football isn't better than the endless Big Brother screenings which are being rammed down our throats at the moment.

My last letter ended with me going to bell-ringing lessons. Did anyone give it any thought? Quite an extraordinary pastime! Our local parish, which happens to be part of the Lancaster Castle, has a bell tower with eight fully restored bells. Each person gets to ring one of the eight bells in a certain sequence. These bells are enormous, the one I was given to ring was as heavy as a Volkswagen Beetle, the biggest bell is as heavy as a Range Rover (I think my trainer, the head of the Bell-Ringers Association of Lancaster, is also a bit of a car enthusiast). Bell-ringing enthusiasts travel all over the country, and sometimes even internationally, ringing bells at various Cathedrals. The talk is: "I rang at Coventry Cathedral", "That's nothing, you should go to York minster, they have 2 octaves of 16 bells there!'" "My aim is to ring at St Paul's", and so on. Some have been ringing for 52 years! What an eccentric bunch.

Anyway, bell ringing practice every Monday night and 'Real-Ringing' on Sunday mornings, weddings, Christmas, New year and when the Queen visits. Sadly, and very oddly, the Lancaster Castle, which is still a working prison, has said that the prisoners are complaining about the noise the bells make (it might be since I joined), so we may have to stop *ringin' them bells* for the sake of the prisoners wanting to sleep in on a Sunday morning. That's what we call 'Human Rights'.

I have also been involved in the 'Friends of the Grand Theatre Group'. Another odd lot of people. The Grand Theatre in Lancaster was built in 1782 and still stands – an absolutely GRAND building. A few years ago, the Town Council wanted to demolish it because it wasn't being used as a theatre, and was not allowed to be used as anything else. The Friends of the Grand decided to try and keep it open, by staging various productions on a weekly basis. Some productions are by professional visiting groups, some are school plays, amateur dramatic societies and so on. However, if there is no-one booked in the theatre for a period of time, we have to put something on the stage – anything! Perhaps I'll read some poetry reading, or tap dancing … As long as it is a production for the public – otherwise the theatre will be closed and, God forbid, demolished. What a joy to work with such colourful characters.

What I love most about British people is their unfaltering devotion to a cause. I sometimes have to chuckle at some of the do-gooders who stand on the street corners on a Saturday morning, braving extreme weather conditions, collecting money for Animal Sanctuaries, Hedgehog Hospitals, Seeing Eye Dogs, Save the Grand Theatre of Lancaster, etc. They may collect about eight pounds in a morning, but pay the equivalent to park their car! No, it's not the same if you just give the money out of your own pocket....

Another favourite are the road signs: 'Heavy plant crossing', one would expect an overweight begonia to step off the pavement and cross the road! 'Major works ahead', I thought John Major had died! "Queues Likely", when there is not a car in sight (although we must keep in mind that queuing is compulsory for all people living in Britain). Just think what fun it will be if there really is a drought and people will have to queue with their buckets, on a daily basis, to collect water, to water their hanging baskets of flowers or perhaps the begonia crossing the road. I digress, back to the weather!!!!!

Did I tell you about the hosepipe ban? One may not use a hosepipe to water one's garden or wash one's car. For this one needs a bucket or watering can. One may however, wash one's dog with a hosepipe – but not on the lawn!!!!

Enough news from this fair land. I must go and join the rest of England in the sun looking for hedgehogs ... or glow worms.

Until next time.

Michael and Felicity

Back To Tashkent

Dear Friends,

Well, the rumour-mill has been tried and tested and I am pleased to report that it is in good working order. For those of you who don't know – I am writing this from Tashkent.... yes, Tashkent! One of the reasons for the lateness of this newsletter is my lack of inspiration: while England is country of very eccentric people, Uzbekistan is also funny but causes one to shake one's head in disbelief rather than laugh. As I sit in my strait-jacket, I may not be able to be as frank as I'd like to be, you need to read between the lines if you can.

It was rather surreal returning to the house that I had not lived in for many years – a bit like the movie with Mel Gibson called *Forever Young* where the main character was frozen for a few years and then thawed back to life, nothing had changed. Tashkent, except for a few new cleverly placed mirror facades on old soviet buildings, also remains unchanged.

The roads the President frequents have been resurfaced a few times, and with each layer (about 10cm thick); the roads have been raised to about second floor level so far. We have about ten years to go before Tashkent becomes a 'sunken city'. The roads the plebs frequent now have potholes so deep they are about at basement level so far. Thank goodness larger cars are becoming more fashionable, smaller ones are disappearing in the potholes!

Speaking of driving, I have decided to opt for the luxury of a driver for two reasons: I do not want to get into my bad driving habits again, they cost me too much in England and secondly, if I drive on the streets of Tashkent like I did in England I am bound to have a major accident sooner or later. The concept of 'polite on the roads' is not understood here. Besides, having a driver (who also happens to be a very good-looking bodyguard) makes me feel a bit like a princess. The only downside is he only speaks Russian and I don't know Russian. The result, my destinations are limited to my vocabulary: school, home, one shop and the gym. My goal is to increase my vocab so that I can move around more. Watch this space...

I miss the Radio, TV and newspapers we enjoyed so much in England. In Uzbekistan we are limited to BBC world, Russian TV and Uzbek TV which is a great channel if you are into Uzbek traditional music and dancing or farming and factory news.

While I have never been a lover of Uzbek food, it is a joy to eat tomatoes that look and taste like tomatoes. The markets are bursting with mountains of colourful fruit and vegetables, spices and oooooh, the bread: soft, warm, fresh, temptingly delicious Uzbek *non* (as they call it) spread with unadulterated butter and honey – it beats a cream tea in the Lake District hands down ....or does it? I think it may have the same calorie-value – a heat-attack on a plate.

After my terrible teaching experiences in English schools one would have thought that I would have stayed far away from this profession – this however, is not the case. I am teaching High School English at Tashkent International School as well as running the library located in a wonderful new facility. I feel more comfortable there because: there are fewer students in each class, the students do not threaten to beat me up, I don't have to bring my own coffee or tea from home, I don't have to worry about using somebody else's teacup in the staffroom, I know the names of my students, and I have not heard F***@* since I left England. Students may be hollering the equivalent words in another language, but I am blissfully ignorant. I love it!

It has been amazing to discover how transient an expat community can be. Most of my friends have moved on to greener (and more interesting) pastures with shopping malls, cinemas, beaches (there is no sea here), fresh fish markets (there is no sea here), cute coffee shops (there is no sea here), etc., etc., etc., etc. On my return I find that I know very few people from the foreign community. I have managed to find an expat choir and we are already performing our first concert with Christmas songs next week. I suppose I should treat it like a new posting – start from the beginning and make new friends. On the other hand, most of my local friends remain the same, less hair, more children and a bit rounder (like me). It's good to see them all again.

Michael misses his life as a student, don't we all!! We're off to his graduation ceremony on 13 December. Life has been a bit stressful for him because the President has decided to give all foreign businesses a very hard time – mining (South Africa's forte) included. We wait to see what happens. His diplomatic activities continue unabated with South Africans interested in doing business in this part of the world. Ahhhh the world of diplomacy… Uzbek businessmen also travel to South Africa from time to time – he even issued visas to a delegation of Uzbek Citizens attending a Bubble-gum Conference in Johannesburg! I kid you not!

Well, it's time for me to close this letter. I will soon know if I overstepped the line in terms of what I should have written about and what not. If you want a good idea of the country I am living in, watch a film called *Borat*, recently released.

No bell-ringing for me, no Grand Theatre, no Fawlty Towers and no fish and chips - just a gripping evening of *Borsch* (cabbage and beetroot soup) BBC and a rundown of the latest cotton prices on TV.

Until next time

Felicity (and Michael, of course)

Dear Friends,

It was a day in December last year that the Director of our school called me into his office and asked, "what kind of risk-taker are you?" Well, needless to say, this question took me by surprise...after all, aren't librarians supposed to be calm and collected, "all-together-type" people? Taking risks just isn't part of our job description! He then went on to explain the situation: "A US Department of Defence School in Germany closed down last summer and their entire library is available to anyone who is willing to pay for the transportation of the books."

Now this, for any librarian, is wonderful news – more books!!!!! We can never have enough books, can we?

"The risk is, we have no idea what will be inside the container," he continued.

After a short time of consideration, we decided to go ahead and transport the books to Tashkent. After a long journey along the Great Silk Road from Europe to Central Asia we were astonished to find that it was an entire container filled with an assortment of every kind of book under the sun. WHAT JOY for a risk-taking librarian? I would never have thought I would ever be the one to say, "there are just too many books".

Well, after opening the container I discovered that it was possible to stuff millions (or so it seemed at the time) of boxes into such a container. As I began unpacking and sorting, I discovered a wealth of books and encyclopaedia sets, which I, under normal circumstances, would not have bought for the library. By this I mean, the kind of books you would like to have on the shelves but have always hesitated because they are rather expensive. Any librarian would be thrilled at some of the treasures I have uncovered.

Most of my mornings were spent inside the metal container, up to my elbows in books, trying to beat the midday sun turning it into a sauna. Our maintenance men, security guards, some of the senior students, and anyone who looked strong enough to carry a box, were roped into lugging an endless stream of boxes to the library on the third floor. All of them, including me, have developed muscles no gym workout could ever produce.

The greatest challenge of all was fitting all these new books into our present library: more shelving and more space – both of which were extremely hard to find.

Today, the Tashkent International School Library has more than doubled in size, with all the books unpacked, classified, computerized, packed on shelves and enjoyed by one and all. What a rewarding project!

Having spoken about the good fortune of the school's library, it would be fitting to reveal the latter, and no less important, part of our story.

Uzbekistan, a country that is enjoying independence from the Former Soviet Union for sixteen years now, continues to develop day by day. For some reason, however, English books have never been a priority. Thousands of students graduate from universities and colleges each year, with English as a major, without even seeing more than a total five books printed later than 1980. During Communist rule, books were well monitored by the KGB - certain books were selected to be in libraries, most of them available in Russian, very few in original English. The availability of English books in Uzbekistan today remains very limited, partly because of past practices, partly because of cost factors.

Moreover, libraries in Uzbekistan today, operate on systems and methods inherited from the Soviet system – a very impersonal and unfriendly environment. Patrons only have access to a "giant card" catalogue on a "card-catalogue-room" where they have to find the details of the book they require, request it from the librarian through a small opening in the screen that divides the librarian from its users, and return the next day to receive the book. The book may only be taken home in very special circumstances. No opportunity for browsing, no opportunity to page through books and absorb the atmosphere a library has to offer.

Back to my container: much of the container contained books unsuitable for a K-12 school library. What better opportunity than to contribute to the community of our host country by donating the 6 000 remaining publications to this library! After three truck-loads of books were transported from the container their new home, it made warmed my heart to see the students help unpack the many boxes, paging through each book, stroking the covers as if they were made of gold, probably more valuable than gold to them at the time. I, as the only experienced librarian amongst them, was more than happy to spend afternoons with the students sorting and shelving these precious possessions as we shared stories from our respective backgrounds. The generous "leftovers" from this mystery container not only bolstered the library considerably, it gave new life and hope to hundreds, possibly thousands of students in Tashkent, young people eager to improve their English and use it in a practical way.

For us at Tashkent International School, we were happy to be able to make such a significant contribution to the community around us, to be part of equipping a generation eager to learn in a world that is developing around them. What a privilege to sow into the lives of some of the leaders of the future.

But wait.....my story continues......

It never ceases to amaze me how a single gesture of generosity can snowball into something beyond our own, limited expectations. It turned out that the excess books from the university library were, in turn, donated to a variety of schools in Afghanistan this January. Who would ever have thought that books from an American library in Germany would ever find their destiny in the hands of Afghan students who have been denied the right to read under the oppression of Taliban rule for so many years? Students who are hungry for ANY kind of reading matter, education, truth, freedom....PEACE. What a great honour it was for the humble library of Tashkent International School to be a cog in the wheel of international understanding, cooperation and development.

Felicity Timcke

A letter written to the International School Librarians' Association

Dear Friends,

While things in Tashkent seem to continue to grind along at an ever-slow pace with school and the rest, Michael has again, after a few years' break, managed to find himself back in Afghanistan. This is not the ideal, as you may well be aware that the war, to put it gently, is not over yet. What is it that draws him? Thank God it's not the women, there are no women left in Kabul!!

With the tide of time, the allure of Afghan gold has caught the attention of a group of investors who wish to be part of the next gold rush in Afghanistan. As you can imagine there is not much of a rush, however, Michael's connections felt they wanted to be among the first, even ahead of the "starters' gun".

Here is a short account, written by Michael, of the country similar to what was seen through the eyes of the 21st century Byron as he travelled the road to the land God seems to have forgotten. Talking of Byron, if you ever come across a 1937 book authored by Byron called "*The Road Beyond the Oxiana*", the Afghanistan he described is still very much the same.

"As is the norm, such a trip always brings with it the unexpected and this was no exception, both in terms of who I was able to meet and level of fun these people provided.

After arriving across the border into Afghanistan with my hosts the Kamgar brothers who own KAM Air, a private airline, we were taken hunting for birds. Once the three 4x4s that would be part of the hunting party were organized, I ended up being part of a group consisting of the one brother and his bodyguard and an added passenger being an Afghan dwarf - sandwiched between me and the bodyguard on the back seat.

As the hunt got underway the dwarf was offered a beer he gladly accepted. He was then given a plastic two-litre bottle which seemed to be almost his size and proceeded to finish the entire bottle within the next 30 minutes. So there I was; hunting birds in the middle of nowhere, at high speed, with an Afghan randomly shooting at birds. Their hunting tactic is to engage in a high speed chase and then fire at the birds by leaning out of the window. Shotgun going off and a, now drunk, Afghan dwarf who was now seeing birds flying, where before there were none.

I found the whole thing very funny as the last time I went hunting in the desert of Afghanistan, I was with the Catholic Priest from Tashkent who asked me to take him to Afghanistan as he wanted to say mass for the expat Irish community there. He too was forced to go hunting and in his case, even given a gun to hold! So from confused frightened priest to a drunken Afghan dwarf I look forward to my next hunting trip. When I asked if I would have a body guard for the entire trip I was informed that it would be a good idea. The dwarf was offered to me for the rest of the trip, it was suggested that with my South African budget constraints, I could only afford his size.

Needless to say, subsequent trips have been more civilized, flying from Tashkent to Dubai, then on to Kabul, whose airport, for those of you who are old Soviet hands, looks like every other Soviet provincial airport but with the guts pulled out of it. After a long passport control session we found ourselves in the parking lot with nobody to meet us, declining offers of lifts from people who, to my travel companion and I, all looked like close relatives of Osama's.

When we finally managed to phone our host, he said he thought we were coming via a domestic flight but I should find the airline staff bus which we managed to find, with three of the air hostesses who had flown in with us. My intrepid fellow traveller did not have to be convinced to join the group of air hostesses, the choice was clear: them or Osama's cousins in the parking lot. This was indeed, a lot different from my previous venture into Afghanistan two weeks earlier with the dwarf and the hunting party. Do forgive my political incorrectness; I am aware that the word is "vertically challenged".

We were taken to our base in Kabul – a penthouse of a newly built office block fitted out in grand style. This was to be our home for the coming week as part of the penthouse office suite doubled as guest rooms. My first stay in a penthouse! Why did it have to be in Kabul? The views of the city from the office, the bedroom and dare I say, the bathroom, were wonderful. The city stretched out before me under a haze of dust, into the distant mountains which seemed to rise up from the city out of nowhere. Some snow could still be seen on the tops of the mountains, which were covered with what appeared to be mud houses. How the folk who live there get up and down I have not yet worked out.

One morning at around 8 o'clock we were having breakfast consisting of the usual fried eggs drowned in a wonderful tasting sauce made of finely chopped onion and tomato dotted with blobs of fresh cream from Pakistan (ouch to my heart). I digress, the penthouse started to sway gently from side to side. At first, "oh oh", I thought there must have been a bomb we were experiencing the shockwave. The shockwave part was right, however, it was an earthquake 180 km away! The building now started to shake violently, making everything outside seem as if it was moving.

What to do? Run down seven flights of stairs or wait and take our chances of falling on top of the building's rubble if it were to collapse. We decided to wait in the doorway of this very shaken building… wait until everything was over. Afterwards I thought how strange the epitaph on my gravestone would have been: "died in a penthouse in Kabul - died as he lived with flair in the land that God forgot".

That was as exciting as it got. The rest of the trip was work which, in these situations, means sitting around in strange offices, being served copious cups of tea while waiting to see someone… anyone! The tea is green and I have begun to take note that the longer it is left 'undrunk', its colour begins to change to a reddish-orange hue. Does anyone out there know why this happens? The nice part of waiting is that one is always given sweets to eat with the tea. I am eating them while I write this and think that perhaps they are only put out to be polite; possibly they have a decorative purpose. Nevertheless, it's late and I like them and I've eaten them all... they will most likely not put them out again when I revisit.

We had a driver whose car would not only unlock as you approached it like most of us have become accustomed to, his car starts without him in it!!! That is hi-tech, Kabul-style. Speaking of cars, there is a sign at the airport that reminds me of where I am in terms of security: "Please switch off your blocking devices beyond this point." The blocking devices are put into the security cars in the VIP convoys to block out the signals that could trigger roadside bombs!

The bank also has a notice board displaying the photographs of the latest suicide bomber who is believed to be in Kabul: "If seen, please do not confront as he is believed to be armed and dangerous".

I write this as my beloved spouse sits in Tashkent biting her fingernails and NOT watching the news. I intend writing more yarns from the country that God forgot. There are countless interesting people who need to be described. Stay well and do not be too quick to choose the penthouse, they are not all they are cracked out to be."

Regards,

Michael (written by Michael)

Pontifications of an Exam Invigilator

After exactly 9 hours and 3 minutes of invigilating high school exams at Tashkent International School, I reflect (as any good teacher or student should do) on my experiences. Yes, I have learned many things. Many things I may or may not be able to use in the future, but indeed, many things about the comings and goings of this room I find myself in:.

I know exactly how many tiles are above the sinks in the science/biology lab. I also know how many footsteps there are between the front of the room and the back of the room – from the window side to the sink side, heel-to-toe as well as separated.

I have bonded with the scorpion in the glass tank at the back of the room, he comes out most mornings to greet me – I will have to visit him from time to time, once exams are over…

I have watched the Grade 9 seedlings grow. I have also watched some of them die.

I know all the assessment criteria for Science and Biology as well as the school calendar on the noticeboard on the wall at the back of the classroom.

In addition to this very useful knowledge, I have also memorized the bell schedule, also on the noticeboard on the wall at the back of the classroom.

I know exactly what to do at the 'emergency eye wash station' at the back of the room - so if you ever need my help…

And just when you think you know everything, Lo and Behold, I got to memorise the Grade 12 report cards, grades, the principal's comments, the teacher's comments. And if that is not enough, I got to analyse them in terms of best to worst, most increased, least increased, best at Music, comparing subjects and so on. This was on the wall in the front of the classroom. What an academic achievement!

I also know what each Grade 12's toes look like, how they write and what the tops of their heads look like. I have also counted and calculated the proportion of left-handed to right-handed people, with a little side-calculation of males to females.

I have mastered the fine art of regulating the room temperature using the air-conditioning controls as well as the opening and closing of windows and curtains at any time of day.

And what power… I have even had the opportunity to stop the grounds man's noisy lawnmowers on the football field with a single telephone call to the head of maintenance "it's too noisy outside, the students can't concentrate; do something!"

It is not only worldly knowledge that I have gained, there are so many things I have learned… about myself.

I have learned just how noisy my shoes are, and that I would rather walk around for 90 minutes with no shoes than spend the entire day in a boring pair of 'silent' shoes. Yes, I was told to take my shoes off because they were too noisy.

Nevertheless, going without shoes was nothing compared to not being able to speak for more 90 minutes! What torture!

I have improved some of my Tai Chi and Yoga positions, learning to balance and focus on a single point in the distance in order not to fall over (this is done at the back of the classroom, of course).

I have mastered the art of sleeping with my eyes open while doing what I call 'the graveyard shift' after lunch. Speaking of which, I have also learned how to curb hunger pains BEFORE lunch.

Patience is a virtue, but when invigilating, it is a skill applied and practiced to the nth degree.

I have hoped with all my heart that someone will need an extra sheet of paper, or a tissue… something responsible for me to do to kill the time.

I have managed to fine-tune the announcements – there are 30 minutes remaining, there are five minutes remaining…. 10-9-8-7-6-5-4-3-2-1… You may now stop writing…

Another thing… I also realized how extremely angry I could get if the person taking over my shift would arrive more than 30 seconds late, 10 – 9 – 8 – 7 – 6 – 5 – 4 – 3- 2 – 1 LATE! Grrrrrrr!

Today, as I enter the exam room for the last time, a wave of nostalgia sweeps over me. I was part of the adrenaline, the nerves, the excitement, the disappointment, the togetherness. Able to give a reassuring smile, a knowing look, a mental "good luck". Exams, in the end however, do have a soul (though most would not believe this). As my last exam, the Music exam, I get rewarded with the strains of Haydn's' symphony number 104, a prescribed work Si Eun (the only student) decided to listen to WITHOUT headphones.

It reminded me of the movie "Shawshank Redemption" where, in a maximum security prison, the inmates are going about their hard labour in the courtyard. One of the prisoners (against the rules) gets to play a love aria from Tosca over the speakers, and all the prisoners get to hear this breath-taking aria as it wafts through the silence of these men as they listen in awe. It is a brief moment of ecstasy, utter bliss… this is what the music exam today did for me today.

By Felicity Timcke

Dear Friends,

There are those who have said, and those who will agree, that working with teenagers is like trying to nail jelly (Jell-O) to the wall. After a year of working with an eclectic group of Student Council members, I can well and truly confirm this. The Student Council, for those who don't know, is a body of students, elected by the students, to organized student-related events and raise funds for these events. Being on the Student Council means that member will develop organizational abilities, build teams, experiment with creativity, practice how to negotiate and develop other valuable life skills.

Confident of their organisational skills (which is why I thought they were voted for in the first place) I started my Student Council journey with the first (and only) civilized meeting. We discussed goals, forward planning, team building, reflection and so on… this was going to be great…. until our first and subsequent events.

Now for those of you who have ever been on a roller coaster ride, you will know what I mean. First of all you allow yourself to be convinced to do this crazy thing, then you stand in line and allow those butterflies on your stomach to take over… once you get to sit on that seat and the safety belt is fastened – there is no turning back!

This is what it is like organising a Student Council event. Meeting after meeting, planning, allocating responsibilities and chores, advertising (always late) chaperones (an extinct breed) and then the roller coaster ride! All the time, having the confident assurance of students telling me, "Don't worry Mrs Timcke, it will all be fine". As the first model walks down the catwalk at the fashion show, or the first singer steps on stage for the talent show, or the first dance is danced at the school dance, or the water fight begins at the picnic, or the doors are locked at the lock in – it all turns out fine in some miraculous way, and at the end of the roller coaster ride, the adrenaline makes you want to do it again.

I have had to deal with trying (mostly unsuccessfully) to find healthy snacks for the candy shop after being accosted by parents at the Parent Teacher's Meeting about the unhealthy (and easy to find, buy and store) snacks that are being sold at the candy shop; dig out accumulated pop bottles from those who have hidden them in their lockers in order to speculate on the return deposit (glass Coca Cola bottles are very hard to find in Uzbekistan. Coca Cola brought in a certain number and not more… with the result, sometimes an empty bottle can be almost as valuable as a full one), dealing with Coca Cola officials complaining about storing drinks other than Coca Cola in their cooler, parents 'forgetting' to fetch their kids from a dance at 11.00pm on a cold winter's night, flooded bathrooms and broken plastic swimming pools (after a spring 'water picnic' which consisted of balloons filled with water, garden hoses and a big plastic swimming pool), making hundreds of salad rolls for hungry footballers, and, how about this, making a candy shop out of a container! My stories are endless.

I must say, I could not have survived through this experience without the support of the ladies (and gentlemen) of the Parent Teachers Association. They have always answered my desperate calls for plates of goodies, support at the fashion show, to hang pictures for the Art Exhibition and to serve hamburgers at the official opening of the candy shop. I should also acknowledge those teachers who offered to chaperone the events attended by the "cherubs" we chaperone at school all day anyway. And last, but definitely not least, I would like to thank this motley crew of Student Council Members who "always managed to come through in the end". How you did it, I honestly don't know – but you did it. Thanks for a great year.

Ms Timcke

"Welcome to Kabul International Airport" the speaker in the plane of Kam Air sounded. The journey was very pleasant: Business class seats, good food, and spectacular views of the mountains… but I was nervous all the way. Apprehensive about being thrust into this "female-unfriendly-man's-world". Armed with a very protective husband and a scarf over my head, I descended the steps of the plane. "Come with me", said a very good-looking young Afghan man. We were stuffed into a 4x4, and driven across the runway to the airport building were we were ushered to the front of the passport control queue. I stood at the window as the rather scary looking border guard flipped through the pages of my passport. I was not afraid; I had my young, good-looking Afghan angel by my side. There were three officials, flipping and throwing passports about like dealing cards for a card game, entering numbers into the computer and scanning barcodes. All very sophisticated for what I was led to believe, a very primitive country.

Flanked by my husband and Afghan angel, we were ushered past the rest of the passengers waiting in a small, badly-lit room for their luggage, to an air-conditioned car, already loaded with our luggage, miraculously! As we drove along the brand-new Turkish-built four-lane road toward the city centre, my eyes feasted on the ironic contrasts I tried to capture on my mini digital camera but was sure to fail: donkey carts juxtaposed with brand new four wheel drives, high rise apartment buildings standing next to dusty Bedouin-like tents, an old, bearded man with his traditional Afghan regalia (turban included) alongside a young boy with the latest Levi 501's and Nikes. The roadside shops were a feast for the eyes, they sold anything and everything, systematically organised into product types.

The building zone boasted mountains of bricks, the wood area stocked wood in every conceivable shape and size, logs, poles, sticks, twigs and more, piled high into the sky, competing in size with the surrounding mountains. The repair shops seemed the most fascinating. It seemed everything was in for repair: tyres, fridges, stoves, TV's, cars, and more... this place seemed to know the real meaning of *recycling*! The gate-welders, I was told, were making good money because of the security situation in the city. Those with money and beautiful houses, had to lock themselves into their fortresses in order not be robbed or kidnapped. "Was this true?" I wondered, so far Kabul seemed like such a friendly, vibrant city.

As we neared the city centre, that nervous feeling returned – butterflies in my stomach. I had not seen a single woman yet! Where were they? Was it true that they were not let out onto the streets? Was I, this western-looking-infidel-American-looking -African-female going to be the freak of Kabul? It was mid-morning and as we melted into the chaotic traffic of Kabul city centre, I started to see them, like the wild game I was accustomed to looking for in the savannahs of Africa: chatting, giggling girls off to school, ladies in and out of shops, women walking in pairs on the side of the road, going shopping or returning from shopping, all covered, some with light scarves, some with fashionable, more substantial coverings, teenage girls with scarves and baseball caps and some with *burqas* (Islamic head-covering) – what a relief! I was relieved about two things so far: more women and fewer soldiers than I expected. Yes, there were soldiers and security guards, each sporting nothing less than a machine gun, ready to be fired (at least so I thought). But not the truck-loads of uniformed men I had become accustomed to seeing on TV news reports.

The traffic, consisting mostly of yellow taxis, each with a 'war wound' of some sort, large, expensive four-wheel-drives, bicycles, pedestrians (who were not even regarded in the bigger picture of traffic in Kabul, donkey carts, busses, minivan-taxis and desperate traffic police, frantically waving their arms at every intersection, hoping to create some order in the chaos around them and, unbelievably so, succeeding!

Suddenly, without warning, we arrived outside what was to be out home for the next few days. To my numerous questions on the topic of where we were going to stay, the answer would always be "I don't know, but it will be sorted." Well, we were put in the executive suite of the "Golden Hotel" located next to the offices of a business associate – Michael's place of work. Again, I was ushered out of the car, told not to worry about any of my luggage, and escorted by the armed security guard to the lobby of the hotel. After much banter in Dari between the men (no women in sight) my curiosity of the topic of their conversation was appeased when they asked Michael, "You sleep together or alone?" At least Michael was able to solve this very delicate problem with a single answer "together – she is my wife". I still don't know if that was politically or culturally correct or not, but I'm glad he opted to sleep with me…!

The deluxe suite came with a sauna, lounge suite, an assortment of three air conditioners (all of which hardly gave us respite from the incredible heat), a satellite TV and a stunning view of the city and its surrounding mountains. Time to relax, catch our breath and unpack was short, before long we were ushered to Mr K's* office next door, a place I had heard about many times from Michael's frequent visits to Kabul. Now it was my turn to enter the "holy of holies". Occupying the entire penthouse floor, this lavishly decorated office, with a magnificent view and home to the successful and well-respected Afghan business man, Mr. K. He is not only like a god, he is a god! He has an entourage of workers, mostly men, who hover around him, tending to his every need: secretaries, bodyguards, cooks, drivers, personal assistants, …all men. A well-dressed, very wealthy looking, very Afghan man greets us with his broad, confident smile. Such effortless hospitality I have never experienced in my life. As we sat and chatted, a spread was being laid before us. Endless bowls of delicious Afghan food, salads, drinks, bread and fruit – effortlessly and unnoticeably carried in from an invisible kitchen! Invited to the table, we shared lunch with this 'god of Kabul' waited on hand and foot by his staff, perfectly, graciously.

We have so much to learn as westerners. We have so many assumptions to erase from our minds. These people: generous, kind, friendly, accommodating, clever, successful and able. Not back-stabbing, dishonest, rude, women-hating, war-loving Muslims! How did the world get to that?

Until my next experience,

Felicity

* Names have been changed to protect the innocent (or me…)

Dear Friends,

As my time at Tashkent International School draws to a close, from my, what seems to be, millions of exam papers that have to be marked, I pause to reflect. Yes, reflecting is good.

Two years ago I returned to Tashkent International School. I returned to a brand new school campus, a beautifully spacious classroom with a lovely view from my window of airplanes coming and going, assuring me that there is a way in AND a way out of Tashkent, as long as you have enough time to be on a three-month-waiting-list.

I was introduced to some of my classes along with the words 'challenge', 'lively'. "Individual" and "interesting". I was also introduced to the new syllabus and I must admit, I have not touched ground since. Under the illusion that English Literature was just the same as any high school course, I jumped in books and all, only to find out that reading the curriculum documents was far more challenging in terms of vocabulary and understanding than any Chaucer or Shakespeare literature I have ever had to plough through. Paperwork at school is a terrible thing.

Surrounded by the 21 novels I was expected to teach for the first course, I started to read (I had only taught two out of the pile of books in my previous life as a teacher). To be quite honest, as I enter the last two days of school, I am only just finishing some of them. Getting ahead of the students, keeping ahead of the students and pretending to be ahead when in fact I wasn't proved to be more of a challenge than ever. As they fooled me, so I fooled them and we made it together!!!!! After hours of discussion, tutoring, threatening, begging and bargaining I was more than proud to see them march down the graduation aisle with diploma in hand.

The notorious Grade 9's scared me a bit at the beginning but we became best friends as they got away with so much – but at least they learned to THINK OUTSIDE OF THE BOX! They were so verbal, hyperactive and intelligent. <u>Antigone</u> and <u>Julius Caesar</u> were a synch in Grade 10, but the most memorable will be <u>Romeo and Juliet</u> – the movie!

My favourite part about teaching English literature to young adults is that you get to introduce them to so much 'grown-up stuff' be it swearing in <u>Catcher in the Rye</u>, murder in <u>Macbeth</u>, and other topics that I may not mention because there may be a Kindergarten student reading this. It is a thrill to be able to gain the confidence of students so that they feel comfortable talking about relationships, fears, passions, problems and other 'worldly stuff'. I think I managed to get this right – we became friends and we chatted more than I taught.

I have had countless memorable experiences outside the classroom too: I have put make up on the faces on boys and girls alike, smearing greasy foundation, red lipstick on their faces and baby powder in their hair just before going on stage for a production of the musical <u>Oliver</u>. I have arm-wrestled with an Olympic arm-wrestler along with some TIS students in Bukhara, I have spent the night on a train with noisy exited students. I have waited hours for the slush machine to freeze, watching it as it froze minute by minute. I have watched the sun rise over the school sitting in the teacher's lounge after a 24-hour lock-in and almost drowned the school after the notorious "water-games" day last summer. I have danced, modelled in a fashion show, made a Romeo and Juliet movie, bounced basketballs at a talent show practice and packed more than 200 lunches for basketball players from all over Central Asia. I have bought more pizzas than I dare to count, enough fizzy drinks to drown the world and helped run a successful monopoly in the form of a snack shop for more than two years. I have sprayed my hair orange, dressed in a "Battlestar Galactica" outfit, walked barefoot down the hallways because my shoe heels were too pointy or noisy. I have laughed, and I have cried.

And I have finally learned how to put my phone on silent….

What I will remember most though, is the concern shown to me by students as I nursed my dad through more than a year of cancer. Returning from long trips home, there was never a moment students didn't ask me, "how is your Dad?" And when he died, the support given to me by these very students was more than moving.

So, as I watch the airplanes take-off and land from my window and realize that soon I will be flying away on one of them, off to make new friends in Turkey, I do not want to forget the friends I have made at Tashkent International School. Thank you for all the fun and thank you for all the memories…

In Zulu we say "*Hamba Gahle*" which means *"Go well my friend"*. The reply is "*Sala Gahle*" which means *"Stay well my friend"*. And with that, I wish all of you the very best for what lies ahead.

Ms Timcke

To my Best Friends and Family,

It's been more than forty sad days and forty sad nights since my Dad died and now I think it's safe (according to both the traditions of my country and my 'adopted country') to stop 'mourning' and get back to living Life. The truth is: one never really does stop mourning. Like a friend of mine said, "You never get OVER the death of someone you love, you only get used to living with the loss". I still miss my Dad very much and always will.

This letter is dedicated to him…

Never having experienced death, except for my grandparents when I was very young and my father-in-law during my first year of wedded bliss, my Dad provided me with an honourable and respectful introduction to Death.

My Dad was a man who made time-keeping his hobby - he loved making time-pieces and his house was filled with many clocks that chimed – synchronised – every fifteen minutes. His habit of perfect timing was carried out right through to his very end: his final three days in hospital gave his family and friends just enough time to visit with him, chat with him, make the usual jokes with him – he even called us into his room one at a time and gave us his last 'good talking to'. There was even enough time for his brother to travel from Johannesburg to be with him for his last few days.

Monday morning: 8.15am, after a hectic social weekend of visiting family and friends (in his hospital bed), a great bath, fresh new linen, his three children by his bedside, his favourite song ('When I Fall In Love, It Will Be Forever") playing in the background, everything said, everything sorted – the beginning of a new week – perfect timing…his last breath, in his sleep… and he's gone …

Is that not what we all wish for?! Well, I certainly do.

Leave a funeral in the hands of two girls and a gal and you end up with an extravaganza of note. My Dad's charge to the three of us was: "I don't want any sour-faced crying people at my funeral and I don't want a long sermon. I want you to celebrate my Life with music and a glass of the best Champagne!"

Well, with this charge, my older sister, my younger brother and I (who probably needed to reserve our energy and ideas for a wedding rather than a funeral) went to town with bunches of flowers, a selection of Dad's favourite music which included an eclectic combination of pop songs such as "Daddy Cool" sung by Boney M, an assortment of other numbers sung by the likes of Abba and Pavarotti, the "Radetsky March" and "Pomp and Circumstance", as well as a short movie of his life screened on the wall of the chapel. Thinking that getting permission to have a garden party with Champagne in the gardens of the cemetery was going to be our greatest challenge, it turned out that convincing the preacher to say what we told him to say and not to preach a sermon was the challenge of a lifetime. He DID (despite countless promises) get a sermon preached, though it was quite short.

This may sound bizarre to you, and possibly even disrespectful. Believe me; his funeral was rather bizarre, yet also very sad. But those who knew my Dad will agree that he was rather eccentric, so a bizarre funeral was very much in his nature and he was remembered for the happy, sociable, optimistic man that he was. I know he would have liked it a lot.

Anticipating that the guests at the funeral would be mostly old people from the retirement village he lived in, we were rather nervous that everyone would share the same sentiment – and not think we were being disrespectful or flippant. Well, it was such a success that a few people have asked us to arrange their funeral for them!!!! What a lucrative business 'designer funerals' could be!

As I said in the beginning, my Dad gave me a respectful and honourable introduction to Death. His affairs were in order and his life was 'tidy'. His Will was in order, every account was paid, he even gave my sister the cash to pay for his funeral! He had no unfinished business, no regrets, no unfulfilled promises, no outstanding forgiveness's, no unsaid compliments... There is so much I can still learn from him, even in his absence.

Seemingly kind words such as "he is now in a better place" or "now his suffering is over" or "we were expecting it" or "it will get better" or "he lived to a good age" are comforting, I find though, that these clichés that we use time and again don't really provide the comfort we expect. Although he suffered from cancer for a very long time, his suffering was shared and alleviated by his family and friends, he lived a good life, for me he could have lived forever, a father is never too old to die. Death comes as a shock, even though you are 'expecting' it and as I said before: I will never get used to my Dad not being here, it doesn't get better - I will continue to miss him.

Thank you to all those who sent their condolences and for those who showed interest and support throughout his illness. It is the strength drawn from friends and family that continues to replace the strength and security I lost when I lost my Dad.

I love you Daddy.

Felicity

Kabul, Afghanistan

Michael, the forerunner of our inevitable move to Kabul, writes this tale:

THE ROAD TO KABUL

"A 1000 mile journey begins with the first step", are the words of some intrepid traveller scribed many years ago. After a number of false starts, my 1000 mile journey began. The false starts meant that I had packed all that I thought I would need in an overnight bag, a tin *trommel* (trunk) I found in our basement that we had bought many years ago from an American missionary, her name still on a sticker on the trunk *Lori Jones,* and my suitcase.

Due to time constraints, it was decided to drive down from Tashkent to Kabul, which all sounds very romantic, but *dit is moer ver* (it is a long way). First we stopped in Samarkand to fill the car and empty ourselves. So far: 3.5 hours, but who's counting?

On we went toward the old city of *Shakrisabs (*the birthplace of Amir Temur also known as Tamerlane*),* a wonderful road that brings you from the escarpment down to the valley below. The very twisty road with great views on the way down had a restaurant on the way, resulting in the decision to stop to enjoy a meal. To my great surprise and delight, I realized that we had stopped at the same place where, 6 years ago, I stopped with Felicity's father and friends on our way to visit the ancient Shakrisabs. It must be the only restaurant in the area.

A city that was the first home of the famous Central Asian leader, *Amir Temur,* was later moved by the leader up the hill, to, what he chose to be, Samarkand. Interestingly enough, one can visit the grave he prepared for himself here. However due to the capital being moved, a new site was chosen and this grave was never used. We do not linger long and once again, hit the road.

A road whose condition gets worse and worse - it seems very little has been done out here in the cut backs in terms of road repair since the days of Brezhnev. Even with the 4x4 Lexus you feel the bumps and all. Six hours later, Termiz, the border city between Uzbekistan and Afghanistan, is ours. We overnight and, after an early morning meeting, we will continue.

All the baggage is repacked into the Afghan registered car for the border crossing and we say farewell to our driver and faithful car. Once more, the large 'logistics metal key' in the form of what has been called the Friendship Bridge comes into view. All passport and customs pleasantries over with, we drive down to the 'big key'. I had noticed in the morning at our meeting, which was at the he port of Termiz, that this 'symbol of love and understanding' had a problem. From the Uzbek and Afghan side the bridge had been painted white, but the two middle sections had not been done. Clearly this is no-man's land (bridge) so it gets none.

Well, back to the journey which takes us to an oil refinery that is still in the process of being commissioned. Here, that business is conducted and then hot and full from the usual Afghan culinary fare, our host decides we should all have an afternoon nap on the plump cushions spread out on the floor. It does not take much debate and all are sleeping. I am awakened by the one son, suggesting that I join them fishing. Fish where? From the Amu-Darya comes the quick reply, like you forgot about the river?

On with my costume/swimsuit (my bags are in the car) six men in the car and the body guards holding on to the roof rack, we set off. It is only a 700m, very bumpy, dusty road down to the river bank. On the way we pass through a USSR-truck-and-tank graveyard. The sands of time have buried much of the trucks so that now all you see are rusty metal roofs growing out of the sand.

Now from the fishing vantage point I was able to take great photos of the still-to-be-fully-painted 'key' to Afghanistan's logistics problems. The bridge was about 800 meters from us with Uzbekistan staring at us from the opposite side. All along the bank are the tanks and APC's (armoured personnel carriers) of the once-proud USSRs invading army. They are all half-submersed in their watery graves. When I asked the question, "Why were they pushed in?" I did not get an answer. The Taliban may have done it as part of their protection against invasions from Uzbekistan. To try to stop the banks of the river eroding is the one I thought to be the most likely, but sadly, not the most environmental friendly.

The fishing part of the late afternoon began in serious discussion. Three men were given nets and were soon in the water, one on the bank the other two 15 meters out. The river seems to have silted up and formed a sand bank so the net spanned this newly formed tributary which flows down once more, joining the man river. These three fishermen were going to walk, deranging the net along with them, one on the bank the other two on the sand bank. So the "let's go fishing" turned out to be "let's pay someone to drag a net down the river while we watch." ...well, watching is active, is it not?

Soon this was proving to be actively boring and the water looked brown, muddy, but oh so cool! So we joined the three heroes in the water! Off with my towel and shoes that were now in the hands of the body guards. Of the 1001 uses of an APC (armoured personal carrier), one of them was a perfect ladder into the muddy waters.

The bridge was to the back of us as we three entered the water, pretty muddy. The top bit was warm and a little below, wonderful and cool. We went over to the sand bank and there promptly decided to have a mud bath. Felicity has always said they are very good for one, in which way 'good' I never asked, but now I had no possibility to call and ask so had my mud bath anyway. The mud was cool and thick I tried to do a star, or 'angel in the snow' thing, you know, when you move your arms and legs up and down, lying on your back. No way, the mud was too thick.

Having had enough of that, I left the other two still playing in the mud and waded to the centre of the water way to try to clean up a little. Swimming down the muddy Amu-Darya with army tanks half submerged watching the three fishermen ending their activity seemed surreal at the time. What a journey this has indeed been, from that first step in Tashkent. I found a tank and used it to help me extract myself from the mud. Oh, I venture to suggest that a mud bath, while being loads of fun, did not prove to be any form of treatment for me at all.

The three 'mudkateers' safely on land and clean, but for muddy feet - the way out of the river was again via a tank. They do make great ladders for pulling oneself up and out of rivers as they do not move; they stay put, weighed down by tons of metal in the mud. Soon, making their way toward us, having too extracted themselves from the river, compliments of the USSR, were the bodyguards with their catch.

They brought the net and laid it down before our feet - like in a movie when gifts are laid at the feet of a king. The net revealed the result of our fishing trip: two fish, the size of a size 8 shoe and a few little chaps. Not worth all the effort we all put in. So ends my fishing story. They say every man has a fishing story I never did till now!

The next morning it was time to move again, this time the final leg to Kabul indeed a step was a world away from the world we know. The first part of the road is not all that interesting; one passes through village after nameless village, the countryside is wonderful and green. We are in the first Land Cruiser the host, his son the driver and I - in the follow Land Cruiser are the body guards and my '*trommel* of treasures'.

A puncture gave us a welcome chance to stop and take a photo or two. The first thing that gets you is the silence - no sound which is finally broken by a passing truck, and then again the silence returns to consume you. It is the season of wild flowers, the most amazing red wild tulip heads held high to form a lush green carpet that covers the hills. There are also some sort of pretty little yellow flowers about and then the real eye-catcher: fields of lavender running up the hills together with the fresh mountain air and the ever-present silence - a deposit in the golden memory bank.

The steel belt all fixed, we are off again, the mini platoon retreat to their Land Cruiser and we are off. By the way, when we did stop, the mini platoon was very professional. They immediately formed a fan of protection around us and kept visual as we enjoyed the view and the drivers worked with the steel belt.

The rest of the long road will follow as I prepare to bring my bride to this strange place......

Michael

Dear Friends,

For those of you who thought we might have fallen off the edge of the world… you're almost right this time. I greet you from my new home in Kabul (Afghanistan for those who don't know). There have just been far too many 'trips to Kabul' to not see the writing on the wall: better to live there than to travel its dangerous roads trying to get there.

After a six-day journey, and 12 suitcases of luggage (223kg in total) I finally arrived in Kabul, met at the airplane, on the runway, by an entourage of passport controllers, luggage handlers, drivers and general henchmen. I wonder if the likes of Marco Polo and Genghis Khan took as long, or carried as much stuff with them, or were even met by such a team of enthusiastic Afghans. After lugging my entire life through a variety of at least six airport security checks and possibly as many luggage carousels, I finally stood facing my 12 bags for one last time: me and about what seemed ten Afghan men feverishly discussing how all of my stuff was going to fit into the two Land Cruisers they had been ordered to bring. Raised eyebrows, shaking heads, a garble of Dari and knowing looks (I think it was something that alluded to me being a woman, a foreigner, and simply, too much of a princess) were exchanged between drivers, body guards, airport officials and the rest of the motley crew, until finally, after what seemed an eternity, the puzzle was finally worked out: the humans would go in the one car and the luggage would go in the other. And there began the last leg of my journey to my new home.

Christmas day for us, the weekly day off for Afghan people – the streets are empty, dusty, interesting, dusty, full of potholes, dusty, lined with buildings shot to pieces, dusty, dusty…. oh, did I say the streets were dusty? The streets are very dusty – in fact, everything and everyone is very dusty. I too, will soon be dusty! It has been my experience, when arriving in a new city a person is usually taken to briefly see the main sights such as Sultan Ahmed, Table Mountain, Burj Al Arab, Big Ben and so on. I was also taken to some significant sites: the most recent bomb blast, the one before that, and the one before that…mmm, interesting stuff@>#<.$>.

My new home I will call the 'Ivory Tower' although it is called the Penthouse in the lift (*elevator* for those less fortunate). It is on the 7th floor of the office block Michael works in, in the centre of the city. Michael alluded to this building in a previous brief – it is still standing after the earthquake scare. We were greeted by the cook and the housekeeper (both men) who were very excited to see us, and very ready to feed us with the most delicious Afghan food. The two-roomed flat was immaculately furnished, not necessarily to my taste, but everything was newly bought for the princess and her beau. I am not sure if it is an Afghan-thing, or if it is my imagination: two rooms, two bathrooms (one in each room), two wardrobes (one on each room), two TV's (one in each room)? Michael assured me that the fact that there is a double bed means that we are not expected to sleep in two separate rooms. There is no kitchen, because Princess has a cook!!! The furniture was bought, and the flat decorated by two young Afghan men, the cook and the housekeeper. It seems home décor (my passion) is not a priority here: pink and green towels, maroon carpets, blue linen with a very busy blue diamond pattern, and a coffee table that has water drops etched into the glass surface - I can see myself trying to wipe the surface dry into eternity!!!

The view of the city is unsurpassed – that is if one is able to see through the dusty windows. "Clean windows", item number one on my 'to-do' list. I could stare out of the window for hours, watching the fabric of Kabul pass by before my eyes.

With possibly the most unusual Christmas of my life behind me, I fall into bed, aware of the heavy silence that envelopes the city. All the lights are out by eight o'clock and there is no traffic except for the lonely cars that pass through the police check point just below us.... I think I am going to like it here.

Much love,

Felicity (and Michael of course)

31 December 2008

Dear Friends,

Greetings to all from a much more organized frame of mind. I have unpacked all my STUFF - replaced all the garish items with some pure cottons, linens and natural shades (as is my habit) ... all soon to be grey or brown with the dust.

Since Christmas Day was a bit of a waste in terms of celebrating, we certainly made up for it on Boxing Day: amongst other delicious treats on the 'leftovers' menu was suckling pig, *Malva* Pudding (for South Africans), chocolate brownies and Irish coffees!!! And we're in a Muslim country? My dinner at the 'House of Lords' confirmed to me that living in Afghanistan is a playground for big boys. This is a house occupied by some very large, very burley gentle giants. In charge of the logistics of a security company, these South African and American men seem to live every aspect of life to its fullest. Their house is spotlessly clean with photographs of their families adorning the walls, a very large screen TV with all the sports channels one can possibly think of (even DSTV), a well-kept garden and even a weapons-depository at the front gate! I lapped up every bit of their conversation as it went from when not to go shopping to where to go shopping for the tenderest meat cuts, the best spices, the widest range of beauty products, the most reliable appliances and the most stylish furniture (if there is such a thing here). They told me how to make a roast leg of lamb and oxtail stew. They were also able to talk about the finest details of the tactics of suicide bombers and.... that's when I quickly moved on to check if their reconnaissance was complete in every detail. Thinking it was a trick question, I asked if and where I could get my legs waxed and a pedicure, they were even able to list the treatments given by the Thai Beauty Salon down the road. These men are neither metro-sexuals nor mercenaries, but boy, do they know their stuff!

I love the sound of a city waking up early in the morning… here we have cars, buses, taxis, barrows laden with all sorts of items for sale. From my Ivory Tower I can see oranges, bananas, dates, running shoes, goldfish??? There are even wagons with little stoves that cook the most delicious-looking wonderfully-smelling food. Of course I have been forbidden to eat off the streets. The cook was most upset when I even tried to suggest it. The sounds of irate horns, the drone of cars, the whistles of the traffic policemen whose job I certainly do not envy. If I look out of the window far above the traffic, at any given time, each and every manner of vehicle is facing in a different direction, drivers blowing their horns and waving their fists. If you will excuse the expression, the job of an Afghan traffic cop is like 'farting against the wind' or better in Afrikaans '*poep teen die wind*'. And I thought driving in Istanbul was a challenge…

Languages! Languages! Languages! Here I go again, thinking about attempting to learn yet another language. I have brought with me a CD from a Pakistani vendor who assured me this language-learning system was faultless. I am yet to test it. The thing is: one needs to learn Arabic script before one can launch into even attempting the new language. Anyway, I have to communicate with the cook who is rather highly strung. He came to me on the first day waving his arms and shouting "*Faligee, faligee*". I was finally able to work out that he was rather upset that I didn't put the LONG LIFE milk and the sponge cake into the FRIDGE. There is light at the end of the proverbial language tunnel, however. Just when I thought that Uzbek was a useless language, I find that I am able to communicate fluently with most of the bodyguards who are Uzbeks from Northern Afghanistan. I have in fact, won their hearts, and I think they will protect me even more now that they can understand me. My very bad Russian comes in handy because most people in their 50's and older still remember Russian from the time of the Russian occupation almost forty years ago. Would you believe it, even my very elementary Turkish (derived from the Uzbek I learned years ago) came in handy when I was looking for a washing machine – all the staff in the appliance shop were from Turkey, selling Turkish appliances. Not only did they give me a hefty discount – I found out where I could find a Turkish restaurant – I think I have won *their* hearts.

Having said all of this, I really need to start learning Dari….

As time ticks by, and we prepare to enter 2009, we wish you all of the very best for this brand new year. While we don't yet know what 2009 holds for us, whatever it has for us, let us take it with the finest optimism we can muster. Life is as good as we make it.

Since Afghanistan is knocking about somewhere in the 14th century (according to the Islamic calendar), I am not sure if the coming of this particular new year will even be celebrated. Apparently this is done on 21 March.

Much love

Felicity (and Michael of course)

PS: *the news has been very busy reporting bombing in Afghanistan lately. When you hear or see news of bombs, check if it is in the South – I am not there and you need not worry. Most of the fighting is in the south.*

Dear Friends,

Oooops! I don't have as much time to write as I expected to. Life is getting hectic! What, with Indian satellite TV, the odd trip to the supermarket across the road, and my new-found pastime…

Keeping fit was one of my major worries. Sitting here in my Ivory Tower, with the only available gym in the Serena Hotel which has been bombed three times in a year, I have decided to embark on a personal exercise regime within the confines of my new home. With no hills to walk up and no well-equipped gym, the most creative and practical way to get some cardio exercise was to run up and down the stairs (we live on the 7th floor). This proved to be rather tricky since I had to wait until the entire building was vacated so that people didn't think that I was completely loopy. That lasted only a few days until I found the ultimate cardio-workout: the vacuum cleaner!

Now, being fortunate enough to be a Princess all my life, I have very little experience when it comes to manual housework (I know this sounds terrible, but that's how it is). It all started with my dust-phobia. For those of you who know me well enough, you will remember that I detest having dust under my feet (I know there are others who share this condition). So, after a few days of trying to tolerate the dust, I set off to make my first major purchase: the most powerful vacuum cleaner I could find in Kabul. With 2000 Watts in hand, I have worked wonders, transforming our flat into the only dust-free capsule in Kabul. I digress… I was talking about my workout. With my *Pilates* ball, my yoga mat and my vacuum cleaner, I am able to do an hour's workout every morning starting with 7 *Salutes to the Sun and Downward Dogs* (yoga terms for those less fortunate), cardio with the vacuum cleaner, squats, cardio with the vacuum cleaner, and so on… Now that there is no more dust left in the flat, I will have to move on to the rest of the building and then … the streets of Kabul………

I do manage to get out (just as you think I've lost my mind). I get to go on an excursion once a day, either to the shops, to an expat pub (so far my least favourite). I will be spending a few days as an examiner for an English proficiency test which will be held at a very prominent foreign organization whose name I choose to withhold. Eager to see what the place looks like, the driver, bodyguard and I set off to do a dry run. Kabul can be defined by areas/neighbourhoods… not streets. It really is quite an eclectic city with an assortment of some modern, multi-storey buildings with glass facades, rows of small hole-in-the-wall shops, houses hidden by very high walls, buildings behind barbed wire fences and sand bags, 'normal' houses plastered with mud and speckled with bullet holes, shops with colourful goods displayed outside – it seems the guild-system of trading is still in operation: there are sections of the city that sell only carpets, only fruit and vegetables, only baked good, only flowers and so on. Some of the streets are even known by what they sell for example Flower Street will sell the kitschy flower arrangements that adorn bridal cars in a wedding entourage, Butcher Street will display, chopped up carcasses and random parts of various animals hanging from large hooks inside shops, along the sidewalk and on stop signs, the famous Chicken Street sells souvenirs to foreigners, not chickens… and that blows my theory.

I have once again digressed. Upon arriving at the very daunting gates of this foreign organisation, the driver and the body guard were ordered to stay outside. I was ushered into a very small room and given a VERY THOROUGH body search by a female guard. This, what I thought, unforgettable experience, faded into oblivion when the gates were opened to let me in: behind a wall made of piled-up sand bags, I could see three guns (I think they were machine guns – what do I know) pointed at me, held by three Nepalese security guards…. Their aim, following me across the courtyard, only relaxed when I was met by my host whose acknowledgement of me obviously assured the guards that I was **friend** and not **foe**. And I have nothing more to say about that experience. Hopefully when I return for the examining session I will be met with slightly better hospitality. I suppose they are only doing what they have been ordered to do. I look forward to interviewing some English-speaking Afghan people, it will give me some interesting insight into Life beyond my Ivory Tower.

Speaking of weapons, most expats carry weapons with them. When going to an expat restaurant/bar (local Afghans are not allowed in because alcohol is served) there are 'lockers' at the door. This is for gun-owners to deposit their guns. For a pacifist like me who has never touched a gun, this is a WHOLE NEW EXPERIENCE!!! There is talk of 'gun-etiquette' whereby one is not supposed to wave the barrel of one's gun around randomly – apparently something the Afghan guards do all the time. Their practice is to they open the car door for me to get in and out – gun in hand!

I am aware that my observations are rather optimistic at the moment – I am also aware that the honeymoon will end in the, hopefully, very distant future. Enjoy the positive responses while they are forthcoming – things may change.

Until next time.

Felicity (and Michael of course)

Dear Friends,

This time, instead of talking about myself, I would like to share what I see from my Ivory Tower every morning. We live on one of the corner of a crossroads. Across the street is a mosque, quite plain, its minaret is decorated with stars and moons, topped by a rusty, rather funky-looking pointed structure made out of metal strips. The *Muezzin* (person who sings from the minaret), clears the phlegm from his throat over the microphone from his minaret at 4h30 every morning before singing the Call to Prayer. Other than the coughing and spluttering it is a wonderfully natural and peaceful sound to wake up to. The garden of the mosque, though very dusty, is spotless. I think it will look wonderful in the spring.

Eight o'clock in the morning is very busy. The corner outside the mosque is a taxi rank/bus stop with all forms of transportation stopping and endlessly ejecting a never-ending stream of passengers. The minivan being the most popular form of transportation: each van has a destination called out by a young man who hangs out of the door, seemingly risking his life. Most people alight while it is still moving, and of course, in true Central Asian style, there is no queue, so there is a mad rush of potential passengers each time a van stops.

The traffic policemen have become my favourites: in addition to their 'normal-looking-military-type' uniforms, they wear white police caps and white gloves. They 'control' the traffic with a baton-like instrument that has a disc on the end of it, with some Arabic letters painted in white. I presume the green side says "go" and the red side says "stop". From my vantage point it seems not many drivers or pedestrians adhere to this instrument, I think because it is too small (about the size of a saucer) and the writing and colours are very faded. Nevertheless, their job and tenacity is admirable.

There is a woman, about 35-years-old, who stands outside our building every morning with her two children. Her son, dressed in the trendiest jeans and sneakers, has red (orange) hair. He looks full of mischief – I'm glad I'm not his teacher. Her daughter is cute, usually dressed in primary colours. Both have their book bags on their backs, waiting to be picked up for school. I think they may be in 3rd and 4th grade.

At this time of the morning, most people are rushing to work. Men tend to wear suits: shiny silver suits or very formal black suits with very pointed black shoes are the fashion of the day. One would not want to be kicked up the backside with such a weapon!!!! There are others who wear the traditional 'pyjamas' (as I call them). They look so gracious in shades of white, beige and light blue. Most of the older Pashtun men will wear turbans (some of them made of silk) with woollen shawls draped over their shoulders, beautifully embroidered on the edges. Quite frankly, I don't know how they keep their "whites so white".

Contrary to popular belief, not all women wear *burqas*. To be honest most women don't. Women rushing off to work in the mornings are mostly dressed quite stylishly, very colourfully yet rather conservatively. Black is probably the most popular colour, complemented with a pink scarf, possibly a red mid-length coat and court shoes (sometimes stilettos). I think the rule is that one's backside must be covered twice i.e. at least two layers of fabric. Some of the woollen scarves draped over the shoulder of the women are gorgeous… I simply have to find the source! It seems the fashion for most young girls it to wear black jeans tucked into high-heeled boots.

No city is without its beggars and urchins. The little children who ask for money on the streets are quite resourceful. Instead of begging as we know it (coming from South Africa), they will try to sell you a bar of chocolate (who knows where they get this from). Their persistence is incredible. Once we were in a car and a small child tried to sell us his chocolate while stopped at a red traffic light. Ignoring him, the driver continued on to his destination. I kid you not, when we arrived at our destination, there was the same child wanting us to buy his chocolate!! Of course they want "Dollars", "Euros", or *Chinggum* (translated as chewing gum). They also wash cars – actually, move the dust on the cars, leaving them a streaky, muddy mess.

The area outside the mosque also seems to be a pick-up area for casual labourers. In the mornings it is crowded with men standing around waiting for people who might need them for a day's work on a construction site, cleaning windows moving furniture or something in that line. On the same sidewalk, those who own wagons wait for goods to sell for the day, or possibly for people who would like to use them to transport goods. It is orange, banana and pomegranate season at the moment, so most of the wagons are packed to capacity with this fruit. Other wagons contain mountains of dried fruit, fresh vegetables, carrot juice, kitchen utensils and so on… They are vibrantly decorated with tassels, leaves, and sometimes even a colourful fabric canopy to protect this fruit from the elements.

On the sidewalk, some men are preparing breakfast dishes to sell to those rushing to their place of work or opening their shops. It looks and smells good. Scrambled eggs drowned in a most delicious-looking tomato, onion and pepper sauce. All scooped up with fresh hot bread - loaves that look like the snow-shoes of Laplanders (for those of you who have read stories of Santa and his reindeer). Old men scuttle from shop to shop holding five or six pots of hot steaming tea in one hand and a tray of cups and glasses in another, serving tea to, it seems, everyone in the street.

So, as my Kabul wakes up to another dusty day, I see a blanket of colour, fabric, and movement unfold before my eyes – the sounds and smells draw me closer to a world I am not yet part of, yet long to be.

War?

Rumours of war?
Naaah!
Life goes on here… people go about their business…
People live.
Until next time.

Felicity (and Michael of course)

15 February 2009

Dear Friends,

Today is a public holiday and apparently we are celebrating the exodus of the Russians in 1989. By the sounds of it, most people would have preferred to have been under Soviet rule for the last 30 years than endure the past and present they have to live with today.

By now most you must think we were exterminated by the shoot-out in Kabul a few weeks ago. Well, I am alive to tell the tale, and here is my story:

On the Wednesday afternoon we, Michael and I, the 'Tyc'* (the businessman Michael works for) and his two sons who also work for the company, were hurriedly ushered out of the office to Kabul Airport. We were told that there was to be an urgent staff meeting in Dubai (a branch office) that night. The plane left Kabul at 16.30 for its two-hour flight, we landed in Dubai and, upon turning the TV on in the hotel room the next morning, our trusty BBC and CNN news channels were reporting the shooting in the Centre of Kabul. Call it intuition, call it inside information or just plain luck… the name of the game is to listen, to obey and do not question… the three major requirements of a good Afghan wife. So much for coming from a position of teaching students to question, argue and analyse, what good would that have brought me…. The only analysis I'm doing from now on is Robert Browning's poetry and the like!

Now that I am back in my penthouse, even though Kabul has a few more buildings peppered with bullets, it somehow feels like 'home' – strange, isn't it? Thank you to all of you who enquired about our safety. Thank you for heeding my request to come to my rescue after not hearing from me after three days… actually, the reason you have not heard from me in such a long time is that I have been rather busy …

I continue to keep my little 'capsule-in-the-sky' dust-free. In addition to the cardio-merits of vacuuming and cleaning windows, I have discovered the joys of cleaning bathroom tiles… I LOVE to see dull and dusty tiles sparkle – or is it the wonderful feeling the cheap cherry-flavoured ammonia-rich bathroom-cleaner gives one… it makes me feel soooooo good! This sounds like an advertisement that could be used on TV during "Desperate Housewives".

You may wonder what I do all day. Well, each day is different:

The other day I was called in by "The Tyc" to interview some candidates to be my Marketing Assistant. The funny thing is, I am not even in the Marketing Department and therefore I don't need an assistant (as far as I know). Anyway, being accustomed to 'cloak-and-dagger' stuff, I was happy to oblige. So my day was filled interviewing people for a job that, as far as I was concerned, did not exist!

I don't get out much. If I do go out, this is how it happens:

I cover myself up with a coat that should cover my bum, loosely wrap a scarf around my head (not a *burqa*), make sure my ankles are not exposed, and take the lift (elevator for those who are yet to learn English) to the basement. The company has about six gold-coloured Land Cruisers, each with a driver and an armed body guard. The body guard wears a camouflage uniform with combat boots neatly accessorized with a shiny AK-47. How effective a camouflage outfit of monochromatic shades of greens depicting leaves and shadows will be in the middle of a city I am yet to find out. I get into the back seat of the Land Cruiser, with great difficulty because the vehicle is so big, the door is heavy because of the bullet-proofing, and of course, negotiating a coat, a scarf and a handbag is rather difficult when getting into a huge 4X4. We drive out of the basement into the sunshine and the busy streets. When we reach our destination, this could be a supermarket, the Chinese "Great wall" restaurant, friends' houses, a hotel, the airport… the body guard gets out, opens my door and Princess alights. He usually follows me to the entrance and then leaves me to go inside alone. .. and that's how it is.

"Why all the security and paranoia?" you may ask. Well, kidnapping is a reality in the city, and sometimes more dangerous than the war itself. Foreigners and wealthy Afghans are targeted with the hope of a hefty ransom. We are foreigners working with wealthy Afghans... and that's all I have to say about that...

I am writing the final part of this letter at the airport on my way to Dubai. The Departure Hall is a sea of interesting sights: turbans, sandals, a multitude of scarves and shawls and woollen wraps, snow-white baggy trouser-suits, beards, green eyes, brown eyes, black eyes set in dark, handsome, faces with chiselled features: high cheekbones and pronounced jaw-lines converging into a prominent, pointed chin (of course all Afghans don't look the same....). Many faces reveal the stresses of their time – the hardships of life in a war-torn country. Most exude kindness and confidence. It's time for afternoon prayers and there are men and women who have placed their woollen wraps on the ground facing Mecca, the more organized have brought their light-weight traveling carpets, others use a random piece of cloth.

In other parts of the Departure Hall are clumps of burly, awkwardly muscular, western men dressed in comfortable khaki clothes with a multitude of pockets on their trouser legs and shirts, talking loudly, in English, on mobile phones. Contracted soldiers? Or is it private security? There are so many terms nowadays one is never sure which are politically correct anymore. Here and there is a solitary businessman, well-dressed in a stylish suit, sporting the latest technology in the form of a Blackberry phone and a kid-leather briefcase, obviously traveling Business Class bought with generously-given donor money – probably the head of an aid agency living state-side, coming to visit those working in 'the field'.

Including me, there are four women on our plane. As the seats fill up with turban-headed, bearded, dark-eyed male passengers, I wonder which one could Bin Laden's cousin, or perhaps even Osama himself…

Naaaaaah, with all those boxes of pomegranates and bursting bags of nuts and dried fruit, they're off to see their relatives and friends, each bringing with them a generous piece of Afghanistan. I wonder how they will be received in their countries of destination…

Until next time.

Felicity (and Michael of course)

*Short for 'Tycoon'

Friday 26 February 2009

Dear Friends,

I went to bed looking forward to a latish sleep as it was Thursday night - no need to rise to early since Friday is our weekend. So, after watching a late movie on TV, I was off to bed, locking all the doors behind me.

BOOM! And the building gives a good old shake, I guess it must have looked like an elephant shaking itself - dust flying all over the place!

Now what? Shall I roll over and sleep some more? Or get up and see what the fuss is all about as I can now hear automatic gunfire as well.

From Felicity's boudoir window I can see thick brown smoke hanging in the air. It is a very smoggy day and a light rain is falling. It seems to me the bomb was behind the Landmark Hotel, close to the Ministry of Interior.

I get dressed and change places, choosing to move to the lounge from where I have a view of the square below and the smoking building. The longer I look, the more it seems that it is near the Lebanese guest house/ coffee shop. CNN and BBC slowly tell the world that their reporters, like me, were "shaken from their beds". But keep saying the Landmark/SAFI was the target.

Ah, but I, the one you sits on high in the penthouse, can see that it is not that building but somewhere close to it. The gun battle continues with the sound of gunfire being interrupted by the odd loud explosion from a grenade or RPG.

Soon two big, bright, shiny fire engines arrive in my square which has, in the last 40 minutes, filled up with what I call *green mambas*, pick-ups (*bakkies*), green with blue lights packed with special task force members in the back.

There is also an assortment of men in police uniforms, traffic police with their white caps and a crowd of plain-clothes security staff, all equipped with radios. It seems they are all talking on their cell phones and two-way radios at the same time.

An hour has passed since my rude awakening and at last the police blockade has allowed one of the loads of ambulances to go down the street toward the sound of the shooting. "BOOM!!!", goes a second bomb in the same area; the dust cloud seems to be coming from the same place.

Shooting is not confined to one area, there seems to be loud bangs and gunfire from further away from the epicentre. The fire engines move into action now, the streets are deserted except for the security staff.

Ambulances are now coming and going down the two streets that lead to the action. And as if from nowhere, loads of press representatives are arriving on foot but alas, as they get to the square they are pushed back and are not allowed down either of the roads that lead to the attack area.

All has being still for 20 minutes when, suddenly, heavy gunfire is heard again. To me it sounds as if they are using 50mm heavy calibre ammunition. About ten minutes pass and then the quiet returns. This stillness has remained until now: 11h45.

The bangs and shooting lasted a good 2 ½ hours...

In the mist of the lull in the fighting I could hear broken glass being cleared away – can you imagine? Then the shooting started again.

What was amazing to watch was in all the gunfire, only two blocks away from the action, folk were going over to the bakery across the street to buy armfuls of fresh bread and walking back home.

I saw two schools girls walking, scarves covering their heads, strolling along as if not a care in the world. Even now, as I type, the sounds of the streets have returned as cars are once again allowed to drive through. The mini bus taxis are loading and off-loading passengers and the street vendors are selling their goods.

The resilience of the Afghan people is incredible to watch, the city centre is back in business: not a beat has been skipped.

Hats off to a hardy people who are, from what I saw today, not easy to intimidate. This might explain why foreigners are targeted these days.

Well I am hungry and am off to make some toast and tea.

Regards,

Michael (Written by Michael)

For those of you who may be wondering – it's not that I forgot about Felicity, she is in another country at the moment.

Dear Friends,

I'm back in Kabul and I must say, disturbingly delighted. It is my home now. There is something warm and fuzzy about being met at the airport by our dashing, handsome Afghan driver, dressed in his white Afghan national pyjamas (I really have to get to know the name of that outfit), his black and white checked scarf around his neck and his rolled-up brown felt Afghan hat. He's young, he's wild and we call him "*windgat*" (an Afrikaans word meaning "Show-off") because of his very dark sunglasses, the way he races through the potholed roads of Kabul but most of all, for his attitude towards anyone in a uniform – in addition to his friendly disarming smile, he has a cocky way of waving/saluting in a sort of "hi-but-be-careful" kind of way. Anyway, I'm glad to see Najeeb the Driver.

Bags in the back, we leave the airport. At the entrance of the airport (about ½ km away from the building), all bodyguards need to be left behind – no weapons near the airport. With the result, the area at the entrance of the airport is littered with guards belonging to the airport, soldiers belonging to all countries who still have forces here, private security guards wearing uniforms of all shapes, designs, colours and sizes, sandbags, camouflage nets, watchtowers and an arsenal of weapons - more than any army in the world will ever need. Needless to say – all these weaponed men are merrily drinking tea, telling jokes and generally having a good ol' time while waiting to be picked up by the people they are supposed to be protecting. This is the place to avoid if something goes wrong... there is the potential of a full-scale 'airport war'. Our body guard jumps in and we're on the road home.

The streets are a little subdued – it is Ramadan here so there are no-tea sellers or food-makers but the roadside stalls are in full swing: fruit wagons laden with about ten different kinds of melon, carcasses and body parts of all manner of bird and beast, mostly cows, sheep and chickens, hanging from the metal meat hooks outside butcher shops in Butcher Street, the wood sellers have their stock neatly sorted in piles according to size, length, dryness and type, they will become busier as winter approaches. Of course what I call the 'supermarket wagons' still sell everything from deodorant to school notebooks to stolen (or donated) army *rat packs* – the ones with the pork meals for Muslims (I kid you not!).

Home at last! It has been a month since I was last in Kabul with visits to South Africa, Iran, Uzbekistan and Dubai – and still, this is my home. It is confirmed with the warm and excited welcome received from our young 'manchild' and our hyperactive cook who is eager to see what I have brought him from all the exotic places I have visited. I unpack the Iranian saffron, the Marmite and a big box of Jungle Oats. Exotic enough? The *biltong* (dried salted, meat) I keep for myself; I think that might be pushing things too far. Actually, Engineer Cook ('Engineer' is a title given to anyone who has education or training in a specialty. Our cook is a trained chef so he gets to be called an Engineer) is not all that hyperactive at the moment – he is also fasting. Nevertheless, he goes about preparing lunch for us fat Infidels – a huge duty and sacrifice – a surer way to get to Paradise. I have since learned that cooks are not allowed to put salt in their food during Ramadan because they are forbidden to taste it while fasting. By not putting salt in the food, mistakes will not be made.

Aaah, home sweet home. Back to my trusty vacuum cleaner, dirty windows and staircase, a workout that can compete with any fancy cross-training-cardio-programme, back to my one-square-km-view of Kabul from my Ivory Tower which is now a colourful spectacle of dancing kites of all shapes and sizes. As I unpack the last of my gifts I place a luxury emerald green velvet box of handcrafted Iranian nougat (*gaz*) tied with a gold silk ribbon on the central table in the office amongst the AK47's for the guards to enjoy at sunset. I still love the stark contrasts of this country.

Now I know this is detailed information you don't want to know, or think you don't need to know but I'm going to tell you anyway... Michael is so stressed he has a carbuncle on his arm. For those of you who don't know what that is, it is a boil, caused by extreme stress, that grows inwardly – extremely painful and extremely scary, especially in Kabul. I looked in my reliable home remedy books for a cure and apparently I need to draw out the inflammation with crushed geranium leaves. Now I have three options: a. to wander the streets of Kabul looking for geranium plants, b. to find a good doctor in Kabul, c. fly to Dubai and find a good doctor. I have found a fourth option: I have plastered it with *Zambuk*. For those who are not from Africa, *Zambuk* is a voodoo, ointment made from special herbs and 'other things' that heals everything. I don't EVER leave home without it.

The reason I bring up the stress factor is that Michael has been responsible for launching a brand new Kabul – Vienna flight for the airline part of the company he works for. No-one will ever have any idea of the details connected to a flight from one city to another, especially one originating in Kabul, going to Europe: catering, security, parking for airplanes, ticket sales, fuel, costing, time slots, connecting onward flights, visa agreements, and, and, and.... There are additional stresses such as narcotics. It is commonly believed that anything coming from Afghanistan is laden with drugs therefore, drug detecting dogs have to also be set in place for each incoming flight. Did you know, dogs that are trained to detect drugs are not actually as clever as we are led to believe? During training they are given drugs and made into hard-core drug addicts – seriously. When it comes to finding drugs, they will do anything to get to them, and that's why their sense of smell becomes so keen: they need a fix!!!! Sad, but unfortunately, true. Anyway, the inaugural flight from Kabul to Vienna will be on Thursday, 17 September – a milestone in the life of Afghanistan. Hopefully the carbuncle will be gone by then.

The sun has set and it is time to eat. People are rushing home to celebrate *Iftar* (the meal that breaks the fast) with their families at home, some have been invited to friends' houses for a special get-together. Others are so hungry they are munching on anything they can find to buy from street vendors who are all too eager to entice hungry fasters with their tantalizing smells of sizzling meat, fried onions and rice *pilau*. Men, mostly those who guard the houses in the neighbourhoods, sit together around steaming pots of homemade food (probably made by their wives early in the morning), breaking long, flat loaves of fresh Afghan bread (we call them mud flaps – those flat rubber things that flap behind car wheels), sipping tea, chatting, philosophising and laughing. Life has been breathed into the streets and they are festively lit up with colourful lights. Later people will come out in the cool evening air to lazily wander the streets perhaps with an ice cream or a cool thin slice of watermelon.

The Mullahs sing their final call to Payer from the minarets, 'our Mullah' the one I can see from my bath in my Ivory Tower, is always a bit late, so when his call is done, they are all done. People will 'boogie' until almost midnight. A bit like Hillbrow (a lively, clubbing area in the centre of Johannesburg) in the 80s, the days before one needed a Nigerian passport to be there. Then it is time to sleep for a few hours before getting up at 3.30 am to prepare and eat breakfast.

It's time to take off my rose-coloured glasses… they're too rosy aren't they? You know, most people here wear the same glasses as I do, they have to. There must be Life! There must be Beauty! And after all… isn't Beauty in the Eye of the Beholder?

Until next time…

Felicity (and Michael AND his carbuncle)

Held hostage by (*Americans)* in my home in Kabul

6 March 2010

It was a 'normal' afternoon in my penthouse apartment building in Kabul Business Centre, on Tuesday afternoon at 2.00pm. I had decided to go out to my tailor to get two jackets stitched. Going out, for me as a foreign woman, is not usual nowadays in Kabul, mostly because of the threat of kidnapping, and of course, the imminent bomb. Nevertheless, this was a well-planned trip, with translator, bodyguard and driver.

The tailor did not take long at all and I was back within half an hour, glad to make it back before the build-up of afternoon traffic.

"What's this! I cannot enter my building? Why not?"

"Sorry Ma'am" We are not allowed to say. No-one may enter or exit. Our orders".

"But I live here!"

Not reaching panic stage yet, I call my husband, who is working in his office on the 7th floor of the same building. Annoyed out of his mind, he explains that they are being held hostage – not by the globally-feared Taliban, not by thugs, not by soldiers, but by an American visitor's entourage. A private American man who thinks he is more important than the others working in the building and can take an entire office block of seven floors, 40 offices and probably about 100 workers and keep them locked in or out for two hours!

The office was not notified ahead of time (too dangerous for the American visitor), there were no exceptions made like issuing temporary passes with photo ID… and no polite explanations. The usual story, we are Americans and we have a job to do so get with the programme.

I was infuriated. I had to stand outside my HOME, risk being kidnapped, ogled by other bored males hanging around me, waiting to be given the 'Go-ahead' to enter my own building.

My plight (as a privileged foreigner living in a very difficult land) was negligible compared to the other people in the building who were finally released, in peak hour traffic, an hour after closing time, to make their way home. A pilot who was supposed to get to the airport to fly a plane was late and the flight had to be grounded.

All because of an *American** do-gooder who was too full of his self-importance to realize that there are other 'normal' people around him.

Do the Afghans really need foreign assistance??

Until next time, if I get back into my home...

An unusually infuriated Felicity

**American* (a person from a western country)*

Holiday in England

Dear Friends,

Visiting England is always a treat for me. Unusual and strange as it may seem: when we discussed our holiday plans for the week of *Kurban Eid*, Michael and I unanimously decided that a holiday in an English-speaking country would be a real holiday for us. We forwent lying on a white sandy beach with lazy white waves lapping from a sky blue sea in Sri Lanka (a place one can get to without the tedious beaurocracy of getting a visa), a shopping holiday in Dubai (never!), a trip home (saving that for Christmas next month), a total workout of the senses in India, or a quiet holiday at home (in Kabul???). England it is: land of "hope and glory", green meadows, fluffy sheep, pork sausages for breakfast, steak and kidney pie for lunch, toasted teacakes for afternoon tea, banger and mash for dinner and polite drivers.

E-ticket numbers and booking reference numbers stored in our phones (remember, we no longer print tickets and confirmation letters in an attempt to save the few trees left on our planet), we eagerly leave the baggage collection area at Heathrow Airport to start our holiday on the 'isle of Mud'. First, off to the Car Hire kiosk with my reference number – a young, pretty English lass sits, what seems to be, proudly wearing her "Europe car" green suit, looking much like an air stewardess, all-inclusive of a mobile phone, covered in pink bling, stuck to her ear. As any other person would say, I politely say, "Hello, I have a reservation to collect a car".

She points in a generic direction towards the door: "bus stop number 18". Not being a first-time-car-renter at Heathrow Airport, I was aware that there was a shuttle bus that took clients to the parking lot on the perimeter of the airport. But being the indignant person that I am, I was insistent that this teenager stopped taking on the phone and gave me the attention I deserved. I stand at the counter politely waiting for her to finish her telephone call…. She doesn't! What do I do now!@#>$#. Of course, being the Princess that I am, I indicate to her that I want to speak to her… she continues, telling me that it is her manager that she is speaking to on the phone covered in pink bling. Well, that was far too tempting for me, "let me speak to him", I say (politely of course).

She leans over the counter placing her face directly in front of mine, "I gave you a simple instruction. BUS STOP NUMBER 18!"

How I miss the older Sikhs, Pakistanis, and Indians who valued their jobs, and (I'd like to think), their customers, who met us with their friendly smiles, polite manners and familiar Asian accents..

Our next challenge was, what we later named her, was Lady Tom Tom – the GPS system that came with the car. The first and greatest challenge was to convince her that Heathrow Airport was not our "home". She was programmed to take us to "Terminal 5 at Heathrow Airport" every time we wanted to return to the beginning.

The next challenge (until we found the volume button) was to hear her directions. She spoke so softly and politely. We drove most of the time without music, the radio and without talking to each other - what kind of holiday is that?

The final challenge for us was to convince Lady Tom Tom that we sometimes liked the country lanes and scenic route – not always the motorway!

Other than that, she continued to be polite throughout our journey, finding new routes each time we went astray, keeping her cool and not accusing us of being idiots, politely asking us to "turn around when possible". Her most endearing feature is the fact that she is able to identify all speed cameras on route. A perfect wife, I would say. I think Michael has fallen in love with her.

My conclusion, a wonderful tool but "are we raising a directionless generation"? There is no longer a need to memorise landmarks, turn the map book in all directions (including reading street names up-side-down), and no more fights about if and when to stop and ASK for directions.

Is it a good thing? Well soon we will wonder how we lived without our dear Lady Tom Tom.

England remains a joy for me to visit. The tiny winding country lanes (the ones Lady Tom Tom knew nothing about), the history, the cute pubs, tea shops and churches… We stayed in an Abbey in the town Roald Dahl grew up in (remember Charlie and the Chocolate Factory, James and the Giant Peach, Esio Trot* and other delightful children's stories).

Even though England has changed much, or perhaps we have become older (and possibly more Asian in our ways – which makes us feel much more at home in England now), it has retained some of its eccentricities:

the postman

the milkman

people reading (and seemingly enjoying) newspapers

dead-pan faces on the tube

overly-polite drivers

painfully slow drivers

detailed BBC weather reports

breakfast shows on TV

charity collectors with tins on street corners in the cold and rain

the guilt of a fully fried breakfast washed down with freshly squeezed orange juice

old people in motorized wheelchairs outnumbering the number of cars on the road on a Tuesday (pensioner's day)

yobs ('boys" spelt backwards), hoods and chavs (Google those)

and, fairly recently, washing out all the bottles, plastic tubs, plastic bottles and trays BEFORE throwing them away in the sorted rubbish bins for recycling.

queues. Thank God, the Brits have still not forgotten how to queue! They have, in fact, taught others to do the same. The queue for the Da Vinci exhibition at the National Gallery went right around the block! After living in Asia and Africa for most of my life – I LOVE QUEUES!!! It is a pleasure to stand in one, assured that your turn will finally come.

My most exciting / eccentric moment was my day in central London: not realizing it, I had chosen to be on Trafalgar Square exactly at the time of the "student protests". It was VERY controlled – quite an impressive show. Uniformed people of all shape, size, colour and rank lined the streets. The Demonstrators moved through the streets of Central London closely followed by at least five rows of policemen in riot gear, and a policeman at five-metre intervals on the sides of the streets. Most-importantly, behind this long procession of policemen – student protesters – policemen in riot gear and television crew, the street sweepers tailed behind, sweeping up any litter with their brooms and dust pans.

Have lessons been learned from fairly recent history? The most disconcerting was the cloud of six-or-so helicopters that hovered above.

London has changed….. but I still love it!

Felicity and Michael (And Lady Tom Tom)

Did you know that is "tortoise" spelled backwards?

Dear Friends,

It is a week short of two years that I arrived in Kabul, on Christmas day. Now we are leaving….

Why are you leaving? You may ask. Well, there are a few answers, choose one that may convince you:

The intervals between the bombs in Kabul have become shorter and the death tolls higher.

And, how safe can you be if the Ministry of Justice and the Central Police Station in Kabul are bombed!

The place I used to work at, was bombed to smithereens and held siege by armed Taliban insurgents (a word that has become part of my vocabulary since being in this environment since I arrived two years ago) for seven hours, killing three of my Ghurkha-guard friends who would make me Nepali tea in the afternoons at 4 o'clock. A strong, black milky tea that was brewed with special spices brought in from Nepal and hidden deeply in their bullet-proof vests. Ghurkha soldiers are considered the soldier of all soldiers as they fought on the side of Britain and her Allies during the First and Second World Wars. They were recently awarded special recognition by Prince Charles for their unflinching bravery. Ghurkha soldiers will fight to their death. This fame has made them sought after by many international organizations that operate in war-torn areas all over the world. I salute my three Ghurkha friends for their bravery.

After returning to the scene of the crime I was more than shaken to find that the entrance was completely destroyed by a 'car-bomb-in-a-truck' that was parked outside. The rose garden in which we sat during our tea breaks was shot to pieces and the wall beneath the room in which I spent most of my time (on the second floor) was riddled with bullet holes. Scary, yet sobering!

My supermarket, "Spinneys" has been bombed.

Many people are leaving.

Didn't Obama and Cameron say the troops are leaving? Well then, isn't it time that I leave too?

There are fewer cars in the streets.

Everyone says I should leave (after seeing trumped-up news reports on BBC and CNN). Of course 'everyone' means those not living in Kabul.

Jenny, the woman who worked for the Aga Kahn Foundation in Kabul, my flute-duet-partner, has left and now I don't have anyone to play flute duets with. And alas, there seems to be no other flutist in Kabul.

The Ivory Tower in which we live is no longer the tallest building in the city, two other buildings have had three storeys added on and now they are nine floors and ours is only seven. One of the buildings is blocking some of my view and I think that's a good enough reason (Yes! If you're living in a penthouse in New York or London!).

The office staff has moved out of the building in which we live so I am the only damsel left in the building during the day, and that will simply not do.....

Now that I know I will not be here anymore, I have been thinking about what I will miss about living in Kabul?

Of course, the lovely view from my window: the minaret, the park, the colourful street filled with carts selling all kinds of interesting goods and deliciously fragrant food.

I will miss the snow-covered Hindu-Kush Mountains that surround the city, ushering a cool breeze in the summer and biting cold gusts in the winter. I will miss the way they silently lie, like sleeping dragons, giving the city a salad bowl effect. They have always been there and will always be there – no matter who comes and goes, the dragons will protect Kabul.

I will miss the 4.30am sound of the mullah calling the faithful to prayer, the shouts of the bus and taxi drivers, the insistent cries of the vendors advertising their wares, the shouts of the traffic policemen over crackly megaphones as they chastise disobedient drivers, the loud beat of Afghan pop music from the souped–up cars of wealthy Afghan teenagers.

I will also miss the whining of the ice-cream-van trying to project a cheery children's tune through its stretched and over-used recording, passing through the potholed streets on a summer's day trying to bring joy and cheer with delicious, freshly made ice-cream with solid chunks of full-cream. A little "heart-attack-on-a-cone".

I will miss the delicious food made by Tufan, our young man-child who, amongst other things, has learned how to cook from an Iranian cookbook.

I will miss Miryam, the crooked, bent-over cleaning lady who is 46 going on 80, who comes in faithfully every day at 7am to shift the dirt from one side of the room to the other and then takes a long nap until it's time to go home. I have always been amazed at how she was able to 'turn on the tears' in an instant, when I was either leaving to Dubai for the weekend, or returning. The problem – I was never sure if her tears were real when she seemed to be mourning the loss of a relative, thus asking for the rest of the day off, or even a few days for the funeral. It could have been true, Afghans have countless relatives.

I will miss the white pigeons that fly past the window at 4 o'clock every afternoon, making their way home to roost on the roof across from our building…. All perfectly synchronized alongside the two troop-carrying German army helicopters that also return home, carrying troops from Afghanistan's hinterland…. Where from, I don't know and don't really want to know.

I will miss the kites that fill the sky in Autumn.

I will miss the gyrating Bollywood movies on Indian satellite TV peppered with very humorous advertisements pertaining only to the

Indian market.

I will, of course, miss the bodyguards and drivers who now fondly call me "Mammie".

I will miss the gentlemen at the 'House of Lords' who are wonderful cooks, entertainers and guardians, especially the gentlest giant of them all who would always assure me after asking him if Kabul was safe, "of course, I will tell you when to leave". I'm sad to say, he left yesterday.

I will miss being the 'honorary man' at all functions, especially at rugby matches watched on large-screen TVs, when the others in the party are dying to say exactly what they feel about the person who missed the goal but are too polite to express their true feeling with words that "should not be said in front of a lady". Is that why there were so many "smoke breaks" outside?

I will miss watching an entire series of Jack Bauer on "24" in real-time. Yes, 24 hours of TV, using advertising breaks for food and toilet stops. Will I really miss that? Naaaah! Once was good enough.

I will not miss the dust! And I will not miss the dust mixed with rain water or melted snow to form a most annoying baby-poo consistency that insisted on sticking to, and packing on to the bottom of my shoes.... Not that I ever got to walk outside in the streets. This annoyance was experienced walking from the car to the front door of the building. I can only imagine what it must be like to walk much further.

Did I say I will not miss the dust?

I regret not getting to do a few things during my stay in Afghanistan:

I am sorry I never met the eight Japanese nuns who have been here since the 1960's. That would have made interesting discussion.

I am sorry I never met the Italian priest based in the Italian Embassy whose job it is to give the last rites to dying soldiers (just like in the movies) and, if they had already been killed, to take their personal effects and the letter that every soldier is meant to carry on their person for their loved ones (wife, parents, lover, children) that is to be sent home after he dies. He would have some sad stories to tell.

I never learned how to play poker dangerously well. That has become the favourite pastime of many people here…. There is nothing else to do, and Bollywood movies become boring after a while.

I am sorry I never investigated the whereabouts of the lost tribe of foreign drug-users who passed through this region during the 60's and 70's and were too stoned to leave. Apparently there are many of them who have settled in villages all over the country – most of them oblivious of the invasion of the Russians, the Taliban, the Americans and others. Wouldn't they be interesting people to meet? That is, if they remember anything.

In a way, I regret not getting to visit Kabul Zoo. I heard it was quite a zoo in its day. Sadly, I think that only a one-eyed lion, a donkey (who fears being fed to the lion), some geese, ducks, a few goats and a host of stray cats and dogs remain. Legend has it that one of the lion's eyes was shot out by a Taliban soldier. For what reason, nobody knows. The so-called religious laws that were strictly implemented by the Taliban regime include nothing about lions having to have only one eye. Legend also has it that the elephant grew too large for its cage and finally died of ……….. who knows what it died of….

Of course, I am sorry I never learned how to speak Dari, or Pashtun.

I am sorry I never got to walk the streets of Kabul. Many say that it was a rocking, swinging place to be in the 70's. People from surrounding areas, especially Pakistan, would come to Kabul for clubbing, eating, watching movies and shopping. The streets were lined with shady trees, trendy shops and girls with mini-skirts. Although many Afghans have told me this, I still find it hard to believe as I drive past the sandbags, metal doors and barbed wire.

As I ponder my departure I wonder if our being here has made any difference. For me and my life, most certainly!

I am more enlightened, I have been able to share my enlightenment with people such as you. I do hope that my insights have made the plight of the Afghan people more real, with less despair and more hope.

Will there ever be peace in this land? Will Afghans always need foreign assistance? Will foreign aid make any difference or should the Afghans be left alone to sort out their own lives? After being here for two years, I feel stronger that the latter is the better option… who knows.

Will Kabul ever belong to anyone? Never! It belongs to the dashing men on bicycles in their silk turbans, the street sellers with their colourful carts and donkeys, the dusty children who sell bubble-gum and phone cards to wealthy-looking people in oversized 4x4's, the dancing boys, the hip young men with their i-phones, the crooked old men with their white beards, the guards in their camouflage uniforms and AK47's, the police, the army, the Imams, the women in their *burqas*, the young giggling girls with their painted toenails… and to the sleeping dragons that surround the city…

All that remains for me to do is to bid farewell to a city that I lived in for two years but never really became a part of. I don't think anyone ever gets to be a part of this rough and hostile terrain, unless of course you're a hippie passing through on the drug trail…..

I will miss this place,

Felicity

Iran

Here follows a brand new chronicle:

One of the reasons for my business (the meaning being *busy-ness*, I DO NOT have a business) is a new assignment in Iran… yes. I would never have guessed that, as I enthusiastically used to read stories about magic lamps, flying carpets and plates filled with coloured rice and aromatic delights, I would have ended up in the land of Persian carpets, veiled women and bearded men… it's enchanting. My assignment involves the English language, lots of people, speaking, reading and lots of words……. English words – some well-spoken and written, and some very badly spoken and written. That's my job.

There are about eight English specialists (I am one of them) who are flown into Iran for two weeks every month to 'make their English magic'. We are graciously hosted by wonderful Iranian people, met at the airport, driven to a 'villa' specifically allocated for us, driven to and from our place of work and fed with delicious delights prepared by our Iranian cook. A most surreal experience – once again, a princess lifestyle in Iran!!!!! Lucky me.

Now this is a country that suffers far too much negative publicity. Despite the information we are bombarded with every time we hear news of this country, Iran is beautiful. The cities are filled with ancient buildings and colourful market squares (for those of you who have access to a map) in Isfahan, Mashhad and Tabriz. Tehran is a busy metropolis with traffic jams, people rushing to and from work while living the normal life of city-dwellers anywhere in the world. The food is unsurpassed, the people are delightful and the plastic surgery 'ubiquitous' (for those of you who have access to a dictionary). Men pluck their eyebrows, women have pouted lips, everyone has nose-jobs and there are no fat people – despite the food being so wonderful. And, contrary to popular belief, nobody glows. The most 'ubiquitous' (the natural teacher in me is just checking if you looked up the word in the first place) past time is shopping: everyone dresses glamorously, even the females who are forced to wear head-coverings and medium-length coats look lovely. I also think that cosmetic retailers, beauty parlours, and plastic surgeons make a roaring trade.

I was privileged enough to celebrate New Year in Tehran in March. It felt quite surreal, wishing everyone a "Happy 1389". This has its own problems. On arriving at 'the villa' the other day, we needed to check through the refrigerator to throw out any food that was past its 'sell-by-date'. Well, try working out if an egg is old if its sell-by-date is 29/1/1389 (and that written in Arabic script). I wish there was a formula to work out the following:

If 21 March is 1 January and 2010 is 1389, then what would 10 May 2010 be in Iran???? Any mathematicians anywhere? Anyway, we decided to put the eggs in water and see if they floated or sank... I read that in a women's magazine somewhere.

This date situation also makes it very difficult when applying for a visa. On the application it says:

date when last visited Iran – 23/01/1389

date to enter Iran – 10 /05 2010   So how old does that make me?

My lot seems to be to have my head covered for most of the time - bouncing between Afghanistan and Iran, what more could I expect? I don't think I will ever become accustomed to this, but there is a certain novelty factor to having to cover your head all the time, I have outlined the advantages and disadvantages:

If you have a scarf, or a piece of cloth nearby, put it on your head like the Muslim women do – it will mean so much more.*

It totally obstructs your peripheral vision. Try looking to your right and to your left without turning your head. YOU CAN'T SEE ANYTHING!!!

Now try driving a car….

Try to drink all the contents of a can of cooldrink, can you drink to the end? Flipping your head back causes your scarf to slip off.

Try to roar with laughter, throwing your head back???

Now try tying your shoelaces???

Or talking on a mobile phone…. Talking is fine, it's the hearing that's the problem.

Walking into the wind with a shopping bag in each hand can become rather problematic.

Scarves slip off you head without you noticing it. It's a bit like having spinach in your teeth, if no-one tells you, you will never know.

 Needless to say, no more bad-hair-days. Wonderful!

Spiky hairstyles? Out of the question. Although, my stiffly gelled spikes help keep the scarf in place, as long as the spikes can pierce through the fabric. Mine do. I find it much easier than those with soft, silk, shiny hair.

A scarf loosely draped beneath your chin could be a handy rice-catcher or crumb-catcher. Particularly when eating a croissant.

For us middle-aged ladies, no more double-chins for the world to see.

Now that I've given you all an activity, I will sign off so that you can get on with experimenting with your head-covering. If you don't have a scarf, try solving the math problem.

Much love,

Felicity (and Michael, of course)

PS: for those of you who have still not looked it up, 'ubiquitous' means ever-present, omnipresent

as I make light of this 'head-covering-issue' I would like to recognise those women all over the world who are forced to wear head coverings – it is not an easy obligation. I would also like to acknowledge those who choose to do so – it is also not an easy choice.

Today's my birthday, no longer a significant event because I'm way over 40, but significant in that it is in a very Islamic country, during Ramadan and on a Friday! Yet another unusual experience to add to the list of "unusual things in my crazy life".

We are currently in the throes of the Holy Month of *Ramadan* (*Ramazon / Roza*) where all Muslims are expected to fast from all pleasurable activities (not only eating) between sunrise and sunset, be serious and introspective, pray and do all other holy things. Thinking I wouldn't survive for more than two days without food, or that I would be shot if I dared eat anything, I set off to Iran with my suitcase bulging with one-minute-instant-noodles, just-add-water-oats, cup-of-soup, three-in-one-coffee and other sustainable goodies. Needless to say, despite some very serious fasters, I have managed to enjoy my usual Persian delights.... only between about 21h30 and 4h00.

Breakfast in a hotel is a little trickier... one needs to order this at 7.00pm the night before. It is delivered to the room the night before and then eaten the following morning before the sun rises. This is done for about a month, until the first sighting of the new moon – those with telescopes get to break their fast sooner than those who rely on the naked eye.

Back to my birthday. Now, being the typical Leo that I am: enjoying being the centre of attraction, basking in the limelight, doing everything in large proportions – I decided that my 'sacrifice' for Ramadan would be not to let anyone know that is was my birthday – practicing (at least trying to) humility and modesty.

I woke up (very early as usual, because of my job) exhausted from not sleeping – my family had been phoning me through the night, one by one, afraid they would not get through to me in this unusually faraway place (and using MTN* – South African mobile phone-users know what that's like). They did… at 2am, 3am 4.30am! Cold breakfast delivered the night before. Off to work. No Internet, no e-mails, no Facebook, no birthday wishes….mmmm. The gods are working together to test my commitment.

Off to the office where no-one knows about me, no more than my name, what I do and where I'm from. Bear in mind that with the no-food-and-no-fun-and-laughter-thing, it is very difficult to order the traditional Birthday cake with candles from the bakery down the road followed by a badly sung rendition of "Happy Birthday", the knife with the bow, the cutting of the cake with a wish for the future and other Birthday rituals that we have become to accustomed to. Being a Friday, which is the equivalent of a Sunday in the world most of you live in – all shops are closed and most people are fasting. There are absolutely no prospects of a Birthday cake. I should have packed a 'just-add-water-instant-birthday-cake' along with the noodles and soup.

I got through the day unscathed and unnoticed, just as planned. … except of course for the phone calls from my loved-ones, my traditional annual birthday poem from my beloved Michael, and a very touching birthday message from my favourite frequent flyer airline loyalty programme.

Now, I know you are thinking "Poor Felicity, she's feeling sorry for herself". Don't! On the contrary, I'm not feeling sorry for myself at all. Actually, I'm waxing philosophical.

Recognition and sacrifice are two very powerful sentiments. I have come to realize that acknowledging someone's birthday is a way to recognize someone for no reason at all. In our busy lives today, do we do that? I don't and I should. So, instead of feeling sorry for me, think of someone who has just had a birthday, phone them and congratulate them.

I have also learned that taking time off to think about things is not a bad thing. Sacrificing something that is important to one's existence is a good exercise - try it. While you may not all want to subscribe to something as severe as Ramadan, self-control and deep introspection is good exercise for the soul.

As you reach for your e-mail and think "I should e-mail her a belated birthday message, or put her name in my birthday book". Don't. Actually, on second thoughts, putting my name in your birthday book may not be a bad idea… who knows, I may be sitting in Southern Sudan next year during Ramadan. Then I might desperately need your messages. Sudan is a joke … at least I think it is …

And that is my lesson for the year.

Now that I have finished a very busy season, I'm back on my soapbox, back in the limelight, back behind my keyboard and ready so write a few descriptions of my most recent adventures. I have had some very interesting experiences and I would really like to share much of it with you….

Until next time… soon.

Your 46-year-old friend,

Felicity (not Michael this time)

MTN is a service provider from South Africa operating in Iran, the word "service" should be dropped from the definition

PS: for those faithful Facebookers, my birthday for some unknown reason, is down as being on 13 August…. It's wrong.

The Only Living Girl in Mashhad.... (taken from the song "The Only Living Boy in New York" by Simon and Garfunkel)

Mashhad is the second largest city in Iran (after Tehran) and apparently the Holiest City in Iran – the seat of Shi'a Islam, holy destination for many pilgrims from all over the Shia Muslim World who make a pilgrimage to Mashhad to pay their respects to Ali Reza who was the seventh descendant of the Prophet Mohammed and the eighth of the twelve Imams (if you have time, look up some of these terms – it is very interesting for those who don't know much about Islam).

The 'resort' where I am to stay alone for six days is a very luscious, elaborately equipped resort just outside the city limits – on a very noisy highway. Surrounded by breezy cedar trees, dotted with fountains and water features, my chalet, one of about 50, is a spacious suite with a small kitchenette, and lounge area and a moon-shaped Jacuzzi-type bath (without the jets).

There is a central reception area at the entrance of the complex, with a dining room and a few reception halls varying in size, used for weddings.

I have a day off so I ask to be taken to the Holy Shrine. One of the girls at the office has to come with me because I am not allowed anywhere on my own. First stop: buy a *chador* (the black cape Iranian women are famous for). Most pictures of Iranian women are of them wearing this cloak, looking like ravens. It looks like the *chador* is worn by most women in Mashhad, I suppose because it is a holy city. Buying one is not at all difficult. The street approaching the Holy Shrine is filled with sellers selling all things Islamic – a bit like visiting the birthplace of Jesus in Bethlehem – Olive-tree crosses all over the place (made in China).Here the shops are full of beads, prayer blocks, prayer books, prayer mats, portions of the Koran written on parchment in beautiful calligraphy and framed in a variety of frame-styles.

Buying a *chador* might not be difficult, wearing one is almost impossible. I have a quick lesson in the shop, but fail. There is just too much fabric… and is so slippery – all it does is fall to the floor leaving me standing, head uncovered, in a pool of black. Besides, two hands are not nearly enough to hold a handbag, hide one's hair and keep the two ends together under one's chin. I resort to using my teeth to keep the two ends together.

"Never mind – let's go to the tailor". My *chador* and I are whisked off into a crowded arcade of tiny shops, through to the back area where there is a small, tailor shop with a tailor behind his sewing machine, surrounded by rolls of fabric. He knows exactly what to do. A length of elastic, about 15cm long, attached to the inside of the *chador* at the top has solved my problem. Miraculously the *chador* stays in place – it's like training wheels on a child's bicycle. Perhaps one day I will be able to develop the necessary skills to keep this cloak on my head without added assistance.

Off to the Shrine. There is strict security at the entrance: women go one way and men the other. We are all frisked and told to leave our phones and cameras behind, wipe off all out make-up (oh God, not my lipstick too!!!!) and hide all our hair (not a problem with my new *chador*).

Through the dark, sweaty, noisy entrance into is a sight that takes one's breath away. A collection of domes, mosaic tile work, marble floors (inside and out), arches, heavily carved wooden doors. The colours are vibrant, the designs intricate – much like the Persian carpets most of us are familiar with.

And then there are the two domes – gold, pure gold – gleaming in the midday sun. It is Friday, and it happens to be prayer time. Truck loads of handmade Persian carpets are being off loaded, unrolled and set up for the worshippers. There must be at least 150 carpets in the main courtyard. There are other carpet-clad courtyards elsewhere. They will be neatly rolled up and stored after the prayer time. The outside courtyard is mixed – men and women – children too. No-one seems to mind that I am foreign, a non-believer, as long as I dress and behave appropriately. I'm a little nervous…

All kinds of people are milling around: old men with white beards, young men with trendy styled beards, crooked old ladies praying for the souls of their children, sick, sad people weeping silently remembering loved ones who have passed, frantic people wailing for an urgent need to be met… I even saw a dead man being carried by six mourning men, covered in hessian, in a simple wooden coffin. The men were chanting portions of the Koran as they walked.

Prayers begin. The courtyard comes to order and everyone kneels. Again, a sight I have only seen on TV and in films. Scattered amongst the crowds are plain-clothed 'crowd-controllers' and guides. They can be recognized by the fluorescent 'dusters' they are holding. We all know these dusters – made of plastic fibres on a stick. They are the modern replacements of feather dusters, brightly coloured in pinks and greens. I imagine they would be good for crowd-control if ever needed. Apparently it is an honour to work in this mosque – highly-educated, well-positioned people come from all over Iran to work here pleased to do the most menial and lowliest of tasks.

We move on to the Shrine: my guide tells me that I am not supposed to enter, but if I pull by *chador* over my mouth and not talk, no-one will notice. This is not a problem for me, remember, I am holding my *chador* together with my teeth!!! It's true, no-one really notices me – everyone is busy with soul-stuff. Some are weeping, some are contemplative, some are reaching out to touch the golden trellis that surrounds the grave of Imam Reza, others are wailing and the more frantic are pushing and shoving. It is mayhem. My guide wants to touch the shrine but is reluctant to because of all the pushing and shoving. Having lived in Asian countries all my life, that's one thing I know how to do well. I tell her to grab hold of my hand I will push her all the way through to the front. We push, we shove, we push and we shove again. All the while she is reaching out her hand above the sea of heads in front of us just in case we get close enough. We do!!! And as she touches it tears well up in her eyes and stream down her cheeks. Amidst all the pushing, shoving, swaying, standing on toes, sweating and desperately clenching my *chador* with my teeth (remember), it was an emotional experience for me too. I didn't get to touch the shrine

I felt it was not my place since I am not a Muslim. People say there are tremendous powers that come from the shrine. I met someone who saw two blind children see....

Now we need to get out of the crowed: we push, we shove, we push and we shove again... at last, out into the fresh air. We collapse onto one of the many carpets out of pure emotion and exhaustion. Zahrah continues to work through her list of prayers. Her family and friends in Tehran knew she was going to Mashhad and one-by-one, they texted her things to pray for at the Shrine. It was her duty to meticulously work through the list. I also did my fair share of praying and reflecting. Once she had worked though her list of prayer requests, we moved on to the next station. This was down an escalator, underground. The most beautifully decorated, serene space I have ever experienced. Perhaps its serenity was accentuated after the frenzy of the Shrine chamber, I don't know – but I wanted to stay there forever. The large expanse was covered in a mirror-mosaic, sky blue, silver and gold hand-painted designs covered the walls and pillars, again, much like the Persian carpets we know. This is a much quieter room, with people sitting around playing, reading the Koran, contemplating, philosophising (is this a word????) and discussing. I loved this room. We sat there for over an hour.

All done, and time to go home... and to let my teeth go of the *chador* I had been gripping with my teeth for most of the time. What an experience. I wonder what Mecca is like????

A girl alone in Mashhad is not such a bad thing. I have come to trust Iranians, I feel safer here than I do at home (South Africa or Afghanistan – what a benchmark). All the people who work at this hotel are men – I have not yet seen a female. These are some of the things that these very kind Iranian men have done for me:

Every evening at 8 o'clock, someone from the kitchen rings my doorbell and delivers me some fruit and a bowl of yoghurt. This is because no-one saw me in the dining room for dinner and they were wondering if I was hungry.

For three days, the resort hosted a conference of about 40 young men. At breakfast each morning, the dining room was teeming with these men, and I was the only female. The waiter brought me an assortment of food from the buffet table so that I would not have to move through all the men to get my food.

Being a tea-drinking country, I get a special cup of coffee brought to me at the breakfast table each morning because, apparently, foreigners prefer coffee for breakfast.

After work one day, I decided I wanted to go to the shop to buy some goodies (also just to get out). I went over to the reception area to ask the receptionist for directions and to tell him I that I was going, just in case something happened to me. Despite being rather concerned, he gave me directions – the shop was about 200 metres away – on the same side of the street. I found the shop, selected some goodies, including milk for my tea and, as I was negotiating payment, the shopkeeper stopped talking to me seemed distracted. He then ignored me and proceeded to talk in Persian to a person behind me. Infuriated, I turned around only to find that the receptionist had followed me all the way to the shop 'in case' something happened to me. They continued to negotiate the price of the things I wanted to buy, he asked me for my purse, took the right amount of money out and walked me 'home'. I followed like a naughty little girl… what else could I do@*#?

One evening, all alone in the dining room, I mentioned (in my very basic Persian) how tired I was of eating meat kebabs (cubes of meat on a skewer, barbequed, and usually very delicious, if eaten in moderation) and asked the waiter if there was anything else on the menu. There wasn't... but the chef was willing to share his vegetable stew (*khorma sabzi*) with me. Delicious!

This may sound like no big deal, but none of this was asked for... it was just done.

Just a minute, I hear the doorbell.... It is a young man bringing me my clean, crisply ironed laundry!

Good night.

Felicity

Dubai

Dear Friends,

With a host of interesting countries behind me, I now face the cruel, demanding, hard-working world of Dubai –a world of glamour, size 8 designer clothes and Jimmy Choo stilettos. What a shock it was for me to shed the baggy robes, long sleeves and disguising scarves of Kabul and Iran, only to discover what was hidden underneath all along. Bulges and dimples that simply do not belong in the glitzy world in which I find myself today…

It's off to the gym for me. Now, for me, the scrooge that I am, I need to pay a lot of money for something like gym membership because I will not dare to miss a day at an institution I have paid so dearly for. No sit-ups on the floor, or following a yoga DVD at home for me….

It was easy for "Edward", the overly-enthusiastic, overly friendly Pilipino boy at the gym, to recruit me. Being of Dutch origin, having a Scottish friend, spending lots of time in Isfahan (all places and people known for their thrift) the free coffee, free DVD rental, unlimited soda fountain, complimentary toiletries, free Wi-Fi and choice of 16 television channels, I was instantly attracted to the value-for-money a year's membership promised me. And that is in addition to the swimming pool, sauna and steam room. Even if I didn't do any exercise, it would be worth attending the gym, just for all the free perks!

My first day: as part of the great one-year membership deal, I get a personal trainer – someone who will "analyse my body" and work out a programme for me. Well, the place is teeming with trainers (it's easy to tell, they have t-shirts with "personal trainer" written on the front and back. The muscles are also a dead give-away). I imagine spending the morning with burly Ali from Algeria, or Ahmad from Egypt or Pedro from Brazil.... Instead, I am assigned to Jimmy from Ireland: a skinny, spindly boy who used to train the Liverpool girls' football team. Can you imagine? Spindly Jimmy, the gym instructor! Just my luck!

After telling me exactly the percentage fat in my body as opposed to the lack of muscle around my bones, the ration of water to matter, sodium, cholesterol and other awful facts I really did not want to know, he set me to work with my tailor-made programme. Being a football trainer I'm sure, most of my exercises are what I saw on TV in South Africa when the World Cup was on in 2010: sit-ups, push-ups, squats, star jumps and the like. At least I only get to see him three times. He shows me what to do and leaves me to plough through my programme…

With my iPod fully loaded with my 80's exercise music in hand, comfortable Reeboks, stretchy leggings, I head for the treadmill – a safe piece of equipment. The lights flash in front of me like the flight deck of an airplane. I press "fat burn" because that's what I'm there for and I press "quickstart" and wow, does it start quickly! I try to keep up, I try to look like I've been doing it for years… I don't think I'm very convincing.

Thirty minutes later, breakfast burned off in calories, things are looking good. Off to the "thigh-eliminating-machine". Trying not to look like the novice that I am, I set the weights and start working at 'eliminating my thighs'. It's not easy getting rid of over 40 years of thigh-neglect. It might take another 40 years to eliminate them. Time passes quickly as I move, and later crawl, from one machine to the next: pressing, pumping, crunching, extending… What makes the time fly is watching the unbelievable fitness and strength being displayed before my eyes. Most of these incredible hulks are like tree trunks – the kind you see on wrestling programmes on TV – with rippling muscles and shiny bodies. And some of them are girls too (I think). They must be lifting weights five times my bodyweight! And that is no joke.

I try to fit in, but my red cheeks are a dead give-away. I am not the only one with red cheeks – there are others there: those who have sat in front of the TV for most of their lives, those who drive rather than walk, those who take the escalator rather than the stairs, and there are those who choose fries as a side dish rather than the salad. Yes, we are all there.

I hold out for 60 minutes, 200 calories, 1 litre of water and 200 percent effort before I crawl to the changing room for my free sauna, steam and shower. My arms are so tired from the "bench presses" that I can hardly lift them to wash my hair with the wonderful complimentary shampoo and conditioner. Steam? Nah, tomorrow! Sauna? Nah, tomorrow! I have no strength left to pull on my "skinny jeans' which by the way, are still too tight. I button my top all wrong because my fingers are too tired to co-ordinate themselves. I try to cover up my red, sweaty face with my wet stringy hair, but without success. I pack my very sweaty clothes into my brand new complimentary "Fitness First" gym back and crawl to the exit. DVD's? Nah! Complimentary coffee, Cola, Sprite? Nah! Free Wi-Fi? Nah. Just get me home, to bed! Oh dear, I forgot about the swimming pool too!

Chiselling away at the rather large *derriere* of mine (which, I might remind you, is an asset in Africa) is going to take time and lots of effort.… It's just as well I signed up for a year. May I bring to the attention of those who are reading this: never take a beautiful-looking butt for granted. Know that lots of time and effort has gone into sculpturing a good-looking body. Next time you see someone, especially if they are over 40, with a well-sculptured figure, compliment them… it's not an easy task creating and maintaining an hourglass figure. And that goes for males and their six-packs too. A word of warning before you decide to compliment: choose the moment, and choose your words carefully – remember, it's not only the thighs and the glutes that have been working out – gym involves arm exercises too.

Watch this space for more about life in Dubai.….

Felicity

It is a Friday morning, the day off in Dubai and I have nothing to do. I call up our old friends in Dubai to see how they are doing; he and his wife have been friends with us for more than ten years. We got to know each other in the diplomatic corps in Tashkent. The world, by the way, is small - they ended up serving their country in Cape Town and now Dubai, so we were able to continue our friendship through the years. Well, that is by the by.

Jay gives me the old line: "so what are you doing over the weekend?" "Not very much", I answer as I consider the next two days in solitary confinement, my beloved being in Iran. "Then you need to come and join us, we have been invited to a *braai* (having lived in South Africa, he knows the correct word for a barbeque)…in the desert."

Yes, I replied, 4x4 s into the desert, a *braai*. A perfect time for a *braai*, I thought, as it is not so hot this time of the year. My wife would have been proud of me: sun glasses, sun block and a hat - full protection against the harsh desert sun - summer or winter. We planned a late start at 10am.

We load the Prada with wine, beer, cognac and potato salad. "Oh dear, we forgot to buy the *boerewors* (South African sausage, especially for *braaing*). No problem, we stop off at the supermarket in Dubai and 20 minutes later, we are on our way again. Yes, South African *wors*.

We all meet up at a petrol station and the three 4x4s head off toward the desert. By now a light drizzle has turned into a hard rain. Of the six days a year it rains, my picnic day seems to be the chosen day. We stop at the entry point to the desert and our host says we will dune-bash for about half an hour, see if the rain stops and, if so, continue with our planned picnic.

I am beginning to wonder why I packed so well as on the seat beside me, I look at my superfluous sun block, sun glasses and sun hat. As the rain now starts to belt down, we follow the other cars. Up and down dunes. For those who have not experienced dune-bashing, it is like being in a roller coaster: going up a dune at, what seems, 90 degrees, flying in the air and BOOM, down you come , then up again, before you can get your breath back – or your backside back on the seat.

The rain stops, but the sun is far from out, so my survival kit is still not needed. We drive to a camel farm nearby to take a closer look at these majestic ships of the desert. Jay has become an expert on these wonderful creatures and I find his passion for them infectious. He walks around showing us the white camels. They are from Sudan; good for racing. Amah, there is a large black camel - they are from Saudi Arabia. The farm had at least 20 babies in a pen - very sweet to see. Jay explained that they are kept away from their mothers as they tend to not know when to stop drinking. They can drink themselves to death!!! Imagine that! By the way they are very loud; I had no idea a camel can make so much noise - a sound like a grunt.

Speaking of grunting, the males are also kept in separate pens even at this farm - tied down. They cannot control themselves with the ladies .The males we saw were foaming at the mouth and at intervals a red sack called a *dull* comes out of the side of their mouth - it looks like a red balloon. Apparently the female camels find this organ very fetching together with their foaming months accompanied by loud roars that permeate the air. Ladies, as they say, "whatever rocks your boat"? This is what happens when they are in *rut* (males on heat). Unlike most males, they only mate for the 2-4 months they are on the *rut*. Google "*rut*" yourself to find out more.

We drove into a natural oasis which has no palm trees, only thorn trees: old and knotted. The farmers cut down the old branches and under the trees were loads of camels eating what seemed to us, dry branches. When we switched off the engines and stood outside all you could hear them munching these dead branches. A unique moment was added to this experience by a very tiny camel, black. Jay explained it was a day old. Camels are born black and change colour within a day, we could still see the umbilical cord.

Our journey continues, in search of a place to *braai*. Once more, the roller-coaster. At last the perfect spot is chosen. The rain has abated for the last hour or so. Incidentally, for the car enthusiasts reading this, the only 4x4 to get stuck was not our Prada, but the 2010 Range Rover.

The desert is beautiful and very quiet - the sand seems to absorb all sounds. I truly heard the sound of silence out there, if you ever get a chance to visit a desert, do it.

The fire took a while to get going with three men attempting to make it happen. Oops, here comes the rain again. A meeting is called. Do we light the fire or go home and finish the, yet to start, picnic there? No, we should stick it out. Two of the cars are drawn next to each other and a heavy plastic sheet is strung between them with the windows acting as fasteners.

The *braai* is placed with a great sense of accomplishment under the makeshift tent. The fire is restarted. The rain continues, joined by a wind. Here we are in the desert, trying to help reduce the wind. Our outside *braai* idea is now half indoors as it lies beneath a not-100-percent waterproof roof with four men who have now taken on the personas of concerned mid-wives assisting with a very arduous delivery.

For the next hour or so the fire is conscientiously tended by the midwives and glowing embers are born. It is now 4 o'clock and Jay's wife suggests, while the potatoes are put on the fire, that we *braai* some *wors (South African sausage)* just to tide us over. This is a great idea and the *wors* hits the spot. By now the wind is really cold and the wet state we were in is not helping matters.

My words when we left the house that morning were ringing in my ears: no, I will wear shorts and there will be no need for a jacket, we are going on a desert picnic in a country that gets rain six days a year. My cap, by this time had found a use, keeping my head warm. As the food arrives at the table, I felt colder and colder and had by this time taken Jay's wife's shawl and tied it around my shoulders. No-one's spare clothes could fit my 'nimble frame'.

Still, the longer I sat, the colder I got. A blanket type wrap was found to cover my legs and midriff as I sat enjoying great food: the tastiest mutton I have eaten in a long time, salads and potatoes. Jay finally suggests that I sit in the car a bit as my now light blue complexion was taking on darker hues.

I was bundled into the car's back seat, engine switched with the temperature set at 30 degrees, and ordered to thaw out at least until most of the blue was gone. I cannot remember when I was ever that cold. This was not what I had in mind. After thawing out I returned to my fellow picnickers. I took the blanket and turned it into a wrap-around skirt - this proved most effective in keeping me warm, however it looked rather odd. A large bearded man in the desert *braaing* in the rain with a skirt and a shawl over his shoulders. Tough times call for tough choices.

What a great day was had to be able to pull off a great picnic in the rain and cold, and not give up, but soldier on. The group of nine never failed in our resoluteness to complete our picnic as planned by our hosts right down to the cake, tea and coffee. Before leaving, which was now night and around 7, we even lit a bonfire, played Arabic music and danced around the fire.

A truly memorable day made possible by folk who did I not melt away at the first raindrop or the last. They had a plan and saw it through to the end. We are home, warm, and I am told, back to my same old colour. All the richer for my **braai** (barbeque) **in the desert.**

'Warm regards',

Michael (and Felicity in her absence)

Part of Michael's job in Dubai is to work with aircraft, all kinds of aircraft: including helicopters. Here are some stories written by him, relating an experience or two:

Minding my own business, as is always the case, sipping green tea, which I understand is good for one's health, thinking of going home as it's around 16 o'clock... my phone rings.

The voice on the other side of the line sounds very stressed - the father of a young man who, together with friends, was kayaking in Tajikistan. An SOS signal had gone up and these men needed to be found. Could I help by arranging a helicopter?

There I was, a South African drinking tea in Dubai and I am asked to do what? My answer was "no problem, Sir, please ask your insurance company to call me I will do my best to make it happen".

I then went to ask my Afghan Airline owner, who also happened to be in Dubai, if he knew any one in Tajikistan who could help. He says, "Yes", and starts calling his representative on his glad phone. At that moment, the phone goes again and it's the SOS Emergency Insurance Company asking for us to help. "No problem, I will do my very best. Call me back in 30 minutes".

So let's see what I want to do with the rest of my day: okay, I will rescue five lost kayakers in the Pamir Mountains in Tajikistan. To do that, I will need to get a helicopter.

To help accomplish this task of getting a helicopter, I have an Afghan private airline owner with me in Dubai who is also instantly committed to the project. He is barking down his gold encrusted mobile phone to Jalil, his man in Dushanbe, Tajikistan.

After what feels like forever, the gold phone gives its "Ode to Joy" ring and Jalil has good news: we can do it, but not now as it is already dark and the helicopters can only fly in daylight.

The insurance company calls exactly 30 minutes later. By then I can confirm we can do it and for how much. E-mails are exchanged, all is confirmed and now we wait for morning.

Meanwhile, five men are somewhere in a valley surrounded by the high Pamir Mountains. It is our understanding that one has a medical condition. Back in the States five sets of parents and families anxiously await news... any news.

Morning breaks and Jalil jumps into action two hours before we wake up. He needs loads of paperwork that is required to be signed off and a huge amount of cash paid as a deposit before the helicopter owners will even think about taking off.

The 10 o'clock departure becomes 1 o'clock... In the meantime I am being called all times of the night and morning for updates on when the helicopter will take off. It finally takes off and we are all impressed with our efforts and hope that within two hours they will reach the co-ordinates and bring the sick person home.

The helicopter gets to the E/N co-ordinates, for those of you who think you have been in the middle of nowhere try to Google this place: 38 degrees 83' 229" E and 72 degrees 86' 038" N.

The helicopters land: they find nobody at this spot, only a broken kayak which is loaded on board as proof that they were there. We communicate the current situation to the US and ask the crew to fly around to try locating them as we are told they are in bright red clothes and carrying 4 bright red kayaks.

No sign... and it's getting dark. The helicopter is forced to return to base declaring our rescue mission a failure apart from the broken boat. The phone rings and a very excited person on the other side says that they have just received a new signal from the ground about 6 miles from the place we had gone to.

I sadly had to inform him that I was no longer in communication with the helicopter and it was being forced back to Dushanbe due the encroaching nightfall.

He would now have to inform the client's five sets of parents that another night would go by in this uncertain situation.

It is resolved to return to the new co-ordinates in the morning and hope they have not moved again. Here is the exact email sent by the rescue company with our latest instructions: it includes a Google Map reference, that way you may take the opportunity to review the terrain.

"Below are the last known coordinates received from the individuals involved in the on-going situation. It appears that they are retracing their steps and should be continuing south approximately 8.37 km, once out of the valley they are currently in we believe they will follow the flat terrain to the east. The flat terrain would simply be easier for the party to continue traveling. The best case scenario would be for the helicopter to go to the last known location below, if they are unable to locate the party at that location to travel south along the valley continuing to search until the helo reaches the flat terrain that begins to wind in an easterly direction. Once at the flat terrain if still no contact has been made if they then could begin following the flat terrain in an easterly direction continuing to search. The individuals involved may still be carrying Kayaks of high visibility and potentially clothing of high visibility."

38 44' 27"N, 72 52' 14" E

Many calls again, all night and all morning, back and forth, also with the US Embassy now having also heard of the problem and requesting to send a person along with the flight. This was stopped by a, "Yes they can come but they will delay the flight as we need to have more documents sighed off if another person boards".

Take off… again. Jalil and his team are on their way. For the next two hours we will have no way of knowing what is happening. Three hours later, the call comes in that they have found the group who, like the previous day, had sent a signal and not stayed in the same place but kept moving. By the way, always remember, if you are ever lost and send an SOS message, stay where you are!!!

The sick one is loaded on board and the rest decide to continue down the river. The helicopter touches down in Dushanbe to be met by the US Embassy in full strength: an ambulance which we had arranged beforehand and all bits and pieces of 'officialdom'. I guess this is the most exciting that has happened there for a while.

Back in Dubai, the Afghan and I shake hands, congratulate ourselves, and continue to drink a freshly brewed cup of green tea.

Relating this story makes me think of another incident that happened three years ago:

I was in Kabul, as always, sipping a cup of green tea as that is what one does in such places, when a Medical Rescue Company based in Dubai, owned by an Aussie rang me saying that they had a problem and could I help. "Yes", say I, before understanding the problem, committing a helicopter crew to a trip, unbeknown to us, we would be talking about for the rest of our lives.

They had a man who had made contact via a satellite phone saying that he was in the mountains and had a heart problem - he gave his co-ordinates. I passed them on to our helicopter ops team who came back with, "this is not a serious request, is it?"

At this point it is time to reveal who he is: a Norwegian, on his own, except his yak, high up in the Pamir Mountains of Afghanistan, collecting flowers! By the way, he mentioned that he was not prepared to leave without his yak. At this point, I did not wish to even think about venturing into understanding this special relationship between the man and his yak...

Our want-to-be-rescued guy had managed to get himself very high up in the mountains, which meant that our heavy USSR helicopter could land but would never take off as the air is too thin up there.

On looking at how to get there, meant a fly through the valleys since the mountains were too high. Going via the valleys meant the endless breaking of international law as they would, at many points along the way, enter Tajikistan airspace then out again and then in again, for both inbound and outbound trips. "No problem", say the Russian crew "*Eta normalya*" (that is normal).

They set off after the price had been agreed upon, the extra fuel tanks fixed while the paperwork was being dealt with. Lift-off and they are on the way. Along the way they decide to stop at a far-off post to refuel in case they end up not finding our target on their first round.

The helicopter finds the flower-picker and his fine looking yak but cannot land where he is. They put themselves down in a nearby village and, on foot, climb to where he is and bring him back. I am not sure how the yak situation was solved, but my understanding was that he/she stayed at the village.

The Norwegian is returned to Kabul via the previous route, once again, breaking international border laws. The medical staff does a preliminary check on him and he is sent to a clinic in Dubai.

The next thing we hear is that he had returned from where we rescued him and is once more high in the Pamirs picking flowers, accompanied by his yak!

The insurance company refused to renew his contract, so if he ever needs rescuing again, we will never know.

The best part of a true story like this on is that one would be hard pressed to make it up.

Michael

Dear Friends,

There is life to Dubai…. outside the confines of the gym. It's hot, it's VERY hot, it's NASTY. As I watch the weather report, desperately hoping for a change in forecast, every single day of the seven-day-forecast shows sunny and 44 degrees, sunny and 44 degrees, sunny and 44 degrees…. This is INSANE!

It's so hot my glasses steam up every time I step outside from the cool (actually icy cold) air conditioned buildings into the hot weather outside. I must admit that I have not really seen much of Dubai to date. Well through steamed-up sunglasses which I can't take off because the sun is too bright, and the fact that no-one really leaves their building during the hot summer months, I have spent most of these sauna-like summer days up in our 35-floor-apartment that overlooks the Persian Gulf. On a clear day, I can see Iran! It is so hot here, the water that flushes the toilet is warm!!! How do I know that? Well, some things we just know…

Food and groceries get delivered to the flat after a single phone call. I don't iron; the clothes get collected for ironing after a single phone call, pretty much everything gets done with a single phone call. How's this? Once I have driven my car out of the air-conditioned parking building attached to our apartment building by way of an air-conditioned corridor, winding myself and my car down 18 floors (I kid you not), I am able to park anywhere in the municipal-marked parking bay and pay for my parking with an SMS from none other than, my mobile phone!!!!

But then, why would I drive out of the comfort of my air-conditioned apartment, into the hot streets? To one of the many shopping malls of course! Many nations have their national pastime, this one's is shopping… well, not really the act of shopping, it is more the act of trawling through shopping malls, looking at what is available to buy, at what could be bought but can't, what should be bought be can't be afforded, what should not be bought but is bought anyway. And then after all these decisions, shoppers sink into one of the many armchairs provided by friendly coffee shops strategically dotted all over the malls, for a cup of something that is chosen from the one hundred options on the menu. That being, if you can find a seat not already filled by the myriads of exhausted husbands who have already been occupying these seats since about an hour after opening time.

One needs a certain kind of stamina for this pastime; a stamina that is not acquired without practice and many mistakes: Firstly, you need comfortable shoes…. but not ugly, not functional, not flat, and definitely not those health-type shoes like Green Cross or Froggies. No, they have to be stylish, preferably platform or stiletto. Then there's the bag. The important part of the bag is that it is not meant to be functional at all. Yes, there must be place for your purse, but more importantly, it must contain all your make-up for quick brush-ups at the many bathrooms that are provided for this along the way. Apparently, because Emirati women all look more or less the same, with their black *abayas* and *sheilas* (black gowns and scarves), their husbands buy them bags so that they can be recognised easily. "There goes my wife with the shocking pink Gucci bag with the bronze detail".

Properly clad, the major challenge is to walk (in those shoes), look glamorous, carry the bag, look at the shops, and do 'stuff' on your mobile phone – all at the same time!! By 'stuff' I mean write SMSs, read e-mails, talk to a 'business partner' or lover. or pretend to do any or all of the above. The point is not the communication the phone provides, it's showing off the latest model of Blackberry, IPhone or anything else that may be the hottest item of the week.

No, shopping is not for *sissies* (the faint-hearted), there are many obstacles along the way that have to be negotiated, sometimes avoided, sometimes used as a tool, and sometimes there are challenges that have to be accepted with open arms (and wallets). I'll give you some examples: on the shopping-mall-obstacle-course always avoid the little Pilipino girls who appear in your pathway offering you promises of delicious food, lots of it, at good prices. Bottomless coffee, eat as much as you like buffets, biggest burgers in town. They lie. This is a method of coaxing you into restaurants that serve the worst food in the mall. Think about it: why would they pay someone especially, give them the infrastructure of a visa, accommodation in Dubai, a uniform, a salary and medical benefits in order to give you good food? Why not hire a good chef? Avoid this obstacle at all costs.

Then there are the pretty girls (usually tall blonde Russians) who stand in the middle of your path, offering you a smell of the latest perfumes This is an obstacle that could be used to your advantage as long as you are dexterous enough to get them to spray it on your body rather than on a small strip of paper that they give you to take with you as a reminder. This will save you having to buy the real thing. If you come to the mall every day, you will always smell nice. A word of warning, blonde Russian women are very dangerous if you have your husband or partner with you… they are a magnet for anything with testosterone.

Obstacles that can be used to you advantage as long as you are shrewd and cunning enough, are the many promises of sales and discounts on the window. SALE, 20%, 75%, 80%. This can be worked out quite easily. Be careful of the sign that says "PART SALE". This generally means as small little bin or shelf in the corner of the shop, stuffed with old, shop-soiled, rejected, broken and very-out-of-date items. It's a hoax! Stay away from these bins. But for the rest, it's fun to dive into racks that are laden with discounted items from the closing season (usually styles that are just about to be launched in other parts of the world), to fight for the second shoe as you sit with the one comfortably fitting shoe on your left foot while some other woman sits with the right foot comfortably clad with the other shoe! Cat fight!!!!

A piece of advice, if you are planning to take your husband, or partner, with you to shop, then, as you arrive, quickly scan the area, making note of all the coffee shops in the nearby vicinity. These can serve as practical pit-stops for tired husbands who need to rest their weary legs and overworked wallets. It also provides a place for you to store all the packets you accumulate from the sale shopping. For heaven's sake, when scouting out the place, DO NOT put him in a coffee shop near the Russian blondes with the perfumes. BIG MISTAKE!!!!

Enough about shopping; although, outside of shopping, sadly, there is not much more to say about Dubai...

In an attempt to create a Dubai that I can relate to, given my travels on the Silk Road, I love to swim in the warm Persian Gulf in the evenings, watching the moon rise over the magnificent skyline of Dubai. I love smelling the sweetness of the Arab men clad in their white *Kanduras* (white robes) and perfectly-placed white headdresses held down with a black rope. The sweetness comes from them smoking flavoured tobaccos in the *shisha* (also known as hubbly bubbly) pipes that are so much part of Arab culture. I love the elegance of the women in their heavily embellished black robes clutching on to tiny little mini Arabs dressed like their fathers in white, or their mothers in black. I love the skyline of Dubai, a playground for architects, creating and fashioning every form of building man can ever think of, and beyond. I love the gardens which line the streets boasting flowers in full bloom all year round. A feat the will always amaze me... flowers and green grass in a desert.

I love the little Moroccan restaurant that we have found, along the beach road, that is so small it only has three tables. But it serves the best lamb tagine I have ever tasted.

"Will you live here for a long time?" you may ask. Dubai is a strange place. It is a place that does not allow roots, like the desert sand and the harsh sun. Nothing can grow here. It is a place that people pass through.

Although there are so many cultures here, working, schooling, living, shopping…. It will never really be home for them, and definitely not me.

As the philosopher once said, "I shall pass through this way, but once…" Etienne de Grellet 1773-1855).

Watch this space for my next stop

Until Next time…

Felicity and Michael

Istanbul

1 September 2012

Dear Friends,

It's Sunday afternoon in Istanbul. It has been two weeks since I arrived in Istanbul with my 400kg of luggage: 41 pairs of shoes (including slippers), 26 strings of beads, 22 pairs of earrings and five suitcases of clothes. Oh, I brought books for teaching too! Of course I did! I really must scale down a bit.

All the new teachers have been treated very well by the school administration with a lovely trip to Troy and Gallipoli, a dinner cruise on the Bospherous, a shopping trip to Carrefour and Ikea, a trip to the bank to open accounts and have a lesson on how the ATM works... why, I'm not sure, perhaps one tends to forget these simple, yet important, life skills...

I have made friends with some of the new teachers and spent the morning with one of them, Tessa, a crazy college counsellor from Florida. We walked down our main street into every shop and bought everything we needed. Things like soap holders, mops, butter dishes and other such life-saving devices. We then had lunch overlooking the Bospherous with the breeze blowing through our hair - exactly what I wanted from a life in Istanbul.

All countries have their own shopping eccentricities but I think I have stumbled across the best of them: ordinary blank school notebooks are bought by the kilogramme, yes, they are weighed like tomatoes or potatoes and the price is determined according to the weight of the books. ALL THE BOOKS ARE EXACTLY THE SAME SIZE AND WEIGHT! Quirky.

I am settling in at school. I have not laid eyes on a single student yet, they all arrive on Monday 8 September. In the meantime we are all feverishly getting ready for their arrival. I'm not so sure what makes them so important, but I try to look as feverishly busy as those who have done all of this before. Important major construction works have miraculously been completed, from piles of bricks and mounds of sand a few days ago to furniture and boxes being moved in to our remodelled classrooms. They are re-landscaping the garden and everything!! I went to bed last night with the gardens all sand and building rubble and woke up this morning to a BRAND NEW LAWN!!!! It must be the Turkish fairies who work in the moonlight.

I have been given my own laptop computer which I am supposed to carry from class to class with all my fancy lesson plans ready to project onto the screen. We are also given lunch in the canteen every day. Mmmmm… dessert included.

Our flat is lovely: light, spacious AND NOISY!! We made a decision this morning to get an air conditioner - it is hot and if the doors are open it is noisy and dusty. Princesses aren't supposed to tolerate noise and dust, especially at the same time…. The flat is on campus, but also on a main street. That way it takes me two minutes to get to school, and there is another door which sneaks me out onto the main street without having to get involved with what goes on on campus.

We have decorated our flat, hung all our paintings - I have even created my own boudoir (a bit like I imagine Barbara Cartland would have – with pearls, furs, silk scarves – not the fluffy white poodle). I have my scarves and beads hanging all over the walls. It may sound extravagant, but I also have my own shoe-room for my 41 pairs of shoes (and that includes slippers). And my supreme luxury: a very large plasma screen TV – I don't even know the size it is so large. Why we bought it – I don't know. I think we got a little confused in the Television shop.

While I have described a close-to-honeymoon-experience there are things I don't like about being here: the noise, the traffic and the heat! Grrrrrr…. Being in quiet, sleepy locations for most of my life has spoilt me and relocating to one of the world's major cities has certainly been quite a shock. This is something we will have to get used to. You will have to watch this space to monitor our progress. Mind you, we have enjoyed the shopping centres, the rides on the ferry over the Bospherous, taxis with meters, and cinemas. I know there is still much more to explore.

On this note I will close – there is still much to see and do. Until next time.

Felicity and Michael

Dear Friends,

It is a privilege to live in such an ancient city. Istanbul, like over the past 2000 years, lies comfortably straddling Asia and Europe. We live in Asia and get to drive, or ferry across to Europe whenever we like, it takes five minutes!

The city itself is a wonderful mix of old and new, state-of-the-art and traditional, there are historical places to visit, modern clubs, restaurants with the latest fusion menus and older traditional eating houses. The shopping is magnificent! There are traditional markets, stylish shops, discount stores, markets, malls and I can even get someone to deliver fresh produce to my house simply by phoning for delivery. This happens when the 'delivery man' calls from the street, I open my window (from the third floor) and lower a basket tied to a rope. He will then place the goods into the basket, I will pull the basket up with the rope, check that everything is correct, and then place the money owed to him (plus a tip) and lower the basket. I love it!!

On Mondays we have a fresh produce market in our street. The entire street is closed off as fruit and vegetable sellers come from the outlying areas with their fresh fruit, vegetables, cheeses, olives, yoghurt, nuts and more. It is a feast for the all the senses. Sellers will not abate as they beckon from their stalls forcing prospective buyers to taste their wares, calling you back if you refuse to buy. It is all very theatrical, very loud, very animated and extremely enjoyable.

Turkish food is unsurpassed. Everything that happens in Turkey happens around the meal table, even if it is only a cup of tea and a toasted sandwich. Some more traditional restaurants will display their mouth-watering dishes in a glass cabinet outside their shops, a maître de-type person standing at the door coaxing hungry passers-by into their haven of delights. Tea shops are dotted all over, sometimes in the most unassuming of places. There is always time (and reason) for a cup of tea. The more elegant, stylish restaurants have waiters like none other I have ever experienced. They watch with an eagle eye from a distance and as soon as the last mouthful is put into your mouth, they are at your side, ready to take away the empty plate and cutlery. It's fun to test their timing as you let the last bit of food hover between the plate and the mouth, without actually finishing it off. A Turkish waiter's nightmare!!!

Turkish men LOVE their moustaches and their hair. Every block, whether in a busy or quiet neighbourhood, will have a barber. This barber will not only offer a simple haircut. A trip to the barber in Turkey will include a hair shampoo and head massage, a hair-cut, a deep shave precluded by a hot towel treatment of the face, a deep shave and moustache trim, removal of nasal hair, the burning off of any ear hair ending with invigorating slaps on the cheeks with strong-smelling astringent and after-shave. This makes walking behind a Turkish man after leaving the barber a very desirable thing.

Turkish men are obsessed with clean shoes. Every street corner will have a shoe-shiner. This is a man, equipped with every colour shoe polish and brush ever thought of, who will shine your shoes in the street. Each shoe-shiner will have a portable stool on which to sit and wait, plus a pair of flip-flops to put on your bare feet as you wait. They take their jobs very seriously… some even boast elaborate brass and wood shoe-shining contraptions to keep their wares in.

In addition to the barbers, the shoe-shiners and the tea shops, we have Turkish men who while away the afternoons playing backgammon, usually outside shops, sitting on rickety wooden chairs around an equally rickety table, clouded in the smoke from the many cigarettes that are smoked all through the game. Apparently the main purpose of this pastime is to get away from their 'demanding' wives.

I have spoken much of Turkish men, but what of Turkish women. Their time is spent, as far as I have been told, is to look after their children (they are devoted to their sons) and to keep the house clean. Turkish women are obsessed with cleaning, especially windows. Many a Turkish woman, will risk her life cleaning her 23rd floor windows, rather than be chastised by family members (mostly the mother-in-law), neighbours or complete strangers who might pass by and notice. Turkish women are so obsessed with cleaning that 50% of the aisles at supermarkets are devoted to cleaning products and materials!

Traffic in Istanbul is INSANE. We have bought a little car (VW Golf) and in order to get to know my way around, I get up at 6am on a Sunday morning when every single Turk in Istanbul is asleep, and practice driving around the city. What makes the traffic so insane is the hot-blooded taxi drivers combined with the tiny roads that weave through the centre of the city. Parking is almost impossible, but no Turk will give up trying to park a car. Even if there is a space EXACTLY the same size as a car, men will gather... appearing from out of nowhere, to help "bounce" the car into the minutest of spaces. Quite a sight! One just hopes that those same men have not returned to their 'demanding' wives when one gets back and need them to bounce the car back out into the street.

I LOVE Istanbul. I love its vibe, I love its energy and I love the fact that it has been like this for thousands of years.

The Turkish-style mosques with their large round domes and spiking minarets that shoot into the clouds that cover the city remind me of old ladies with their large skirts draped around them as they sit – stable and unmoving, just as the Bospherous lies still and unmoving, ferrying people, cargo ships, cruise liners, military ships, fishing boats, water taxis, passenger ferries, yachts and more to and fro, backwards and forwards.

I love this place.

Felicity and Michael

About home....

We, like many others, have been wanderers for most of our lives: pilgrims, expats, refugees, diplomats, call it what you may.

But what do we call home…?

What is my national identity?

As a South African that has lived outside my country for more than 25 years this becomes a complicated issue as one drifts into being a citizen of the world. A world in which some nations have their identity very cut and dried compared to our situation in South Africa. However, I see no point in comparing what others have as a national identity. As each nation brings its unique attributes, the common definition of national identity is to have a sense of belonging, and yes I do have that sense.

My anchor is firm and strong, embedded deep into Africa. The narrative of a national identity is not one in which we need to look at the normal components that made up an identity. Here I am referring to food, music, art and so forth.

In a very multi-cultural society which goes to make up the nation of South Africa I believe I have absorbed all of these to project an identity in terms of what we eat, music we dance to or sing and the art which we enjoy are drum beats, disco, *boere* music, classical music. We are *sheba* and *pap*, *braaivleis*, curry, Sunday roast. We are soccer, ruby, cricket. We are a kaleidoscope of tastes, colours and languages. We are South Africa. My national identity is interwoven in having adopted others' foods colours and traditions.

My South African/national identity is a true patchwork of all the diversities that are waiting to be absorbed by me, making one piece of cloth my national identity.

There are basic fundamentals that make up my national identity as a South African; a country in which all are free to live their lives as they wish, worship their God, express there opposing views while sitting under our warm African sun.

I feel my identity is made up of these values which were hard fought for and won. As a South African living afar, I look with pride when I spot an SAA aircraft at an airport, see our produce being sold in supermarkets around the world.

We indeed do not have one national dish or song or dance and that is what makes our identity our diversity. However we do have common values on freedom, democracy, and the pride of being a part of our nation. A wonderful flag and national emblems which identify me as a South African.

As a South African living abroad I feel secure in my national identity which I see founded on shared values, pride in our nation's achievements including the miracle of our political present, and a constitution that binds us together with our values.

The End

Igor Savitsky:
Artist, Collector, Museum Founder
by Marinika Babanazarova

This is the biography of the astonishing life of Igor Savitsky, who rescued thousands of dissident artworks from Stalinist repression that survive today in the Karakalpakstan Museum, in Nukus, Uzbekistan; a collection of Soviet avant-garde art rivalled only by the Russian Museum in St Petersburg. The remoteness of the area, and its proximity to chemical weapons testing sites nearby, helped Savitsky keep his collection secret while, tragically, some of the Russian and Uzbek artists involved were either imprisoned or executed.

The author is the director of the museum, a post she has held since the death in 1984 of Savitsky, who was a regular visitor to her family. Savitsky's life is vividly narrated through detail from correspondence, official records, and family documents that have become available only recently, as well as the recollections of so many of those who knew this remarkable man.

RRP:£10.00
ISBN: 978-0-9557549-9-9

Friendly Steppes: A Silk Road Journey
by Nick Rowan

This is the chronicle of an extraordinary adventure that led Nick Rowan to some of the world's most incredible and hidden places. Intertwined with the magic of 2,000 years of Silk Road history, he recounts his experiences coupled with a remarkable realisation of just what an impact this trade route has had on our society as we know it today. Containing colourful stories, beautiful photography and vivid characters, and wrapped in the local myths and legends told by the people Nick met and who live

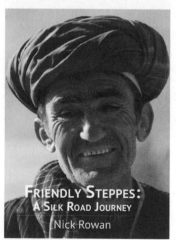

along the route, this is both a travelogue and an education of a part of the world that has remained hidden for hundreds of years.

Friendly Steppes: A Silk Road Journey reveals just how rich the region was both culturally and economically and uncovers countless new friends as Nick travels from Venice through Eastern Europe, Iran, the ancient and modern Central Asia of places like Samarkand, Bishkek and Turkmenbashi, and on to China, along the Silk Roads of today.

RRP:£14.95
ISBN: 978-0-9557549-4-4

Birds of Uzbekistan
by Boris Nedosekov

This is a superb collection of full-colour photographs provided by the members of Uzbekistan Society for the Protection of Birds, with text in both English and in Russian. Since the collapse of the Soviet Union and Uzbekistan's declaration of independence in 1991, unlike in other Central Asian states there have been no such illustrated books published about the birds of this country's rich and diverse wildlife.

There are more than 500 species of birds in Uzbekistan, with 32 included in the International Red Data Book. After independence, Uzbekistan began to attract the attention of foreign tourist companies, and particularly those specialising in ornithological tourism and birdwatching.

Birds of Uzbekistan is therefore a much-needed and timely portrait of this element of the country's remarkable wildlife.

RRP: £24.95
ISBN: 978-0955754913

The Alphabet Game
by Paul Wilson

With the future of Guidebooks under threat, The Alphabet Game takes you back to the very beginning, back to their earliest incarnations and the gamesmanship that brought them into being. As Evelyn Waugh's Scoop did for Foreign Correspondents the world over, so this novel lifts the lid on Travel Writers for good.

Travelling around the world may appear as easy as A,B,C in the twenty first century, but looks can be deceptive: there is no 'X' for a start. Not since Xidakistan was struck from the map. But post 9/11, with the War on Terror going global, the sovereignty of 'The Valley' is back on the agenda. Could the Xidakis, like their Uzbek and Tajik neighbours, be about to taste the freedom of independence? Will Xidakistan once again take its rightful place in the League of Nations?

The Valley's fate is inextricably linked with that of Graham Ruff, founder of Ruff Guides. In a tale setting sail where Around the World in Eighty Days and Lost Horizon weighed anchor, our not-quite-a-hero suffers all the slings and arrows outrageous fortune can muster, in his pursuit of the golden triangle: The Game, The Guidebook, The Girl.

Wilson tells The Game's story with his usual mix of irreverent wit and historical insight, and in doing so delivers the most telling satire on an American war effort since M*A*S*H.

The Guidebook is Dead? Long Live the Guidebook.

RRP: £14.95
ISBN: 978-0-9927873-2-5

The Gods of the Middle World
by Galina Dolgaya

The Gods of the Middle World, the new novel by Galina Dolgaya, tells the story of Sima, a student of archaeology for whom the old lore and ways of the Central Asian steppe peoples are as vivid as the present. When she joints a group of archaeologists in southern Kazakhstan, asking all the time whether it is really possible to 'commune with the spirits', she soon discovers the answer first hand, setting in motion events in the spirit worlds that have been frozen for centuries. Meanwhile three millennia earlier, on the same spot, a young woman and her companion struggle to survive and amend wrongs that have caused the neighbouring tribe to avenge for them. The two narratives mirror one another, while Sima finds her destiny intertwined with the struggle between the forces of good and evil. Drawing richly on the historical and mythical backgrounds of the southern Kazakh steppe, the novel ultimately addresses the responsibilities of each generation for those that follow and the central importance of love and forgiveness.

Based in Tashkent and with a lifetime of first-hand knowledge of the region in which the story is set, Galina Dolgaya has published a number of novels and poems in Russian. The Gods of the Middle World won first prize at the 2012 Open Central Asia Literature Festival and is her first work to be available in English, published by Hertfordshire Press.

RRP: £14.95
ISBN:978-0-9574807-9-7